T0362906

PUBLISHED BY BOOM BOOKS
boombooks.biz

ABOUT THIS SERIES

.... But after that, I realised that I knew very little about these parents of mine. They had been born about the start of the Twentieth Century, and they died in 1970 and 1980. For their last 50 years, I was old enough to speak with a bit of sense.

I could have talked to them a lot about their lives. I could have found out about the times they lived in. But I did not. I know almost nothing about them really. Their courtship? Working in the pits? The Lock-out in the Depression? Losing their second child? Being dusted as a miner? The shootings at Rothbury? My uncles killed in the War? Love on the dole? There were hundreds, thousands of questions that I would now like to ask them. But, alas, I can't. It's too late.

Thus, prompted by my guilt, I resolved to write these books. They describe happenings that affected people, real people. The whole series is, to coin a modern phrase, designed to push your buttons, to make you remember and wonder at things forgotten. The books might just let nostalgia see the light of day, so that oldies and youngies will talk about the past and re-discover a heritage otherwise forgotten. Hopefully, they will spark discussions between generations, and foster the asking and answering of questions that should not remain unanswered.

BORN IN 1951?
WHAT ELSE HAPPENED?

RON WILLIAMS

AUSTRALIAN SOCIAL HISTORY

BOOK 13 IN A SERIES OF 35

War Babies Years (1939 to 1945): 7 Titles

Baby Boom Years (1946 to 1960): 15 Titles

Post Boom Years (1961 to 1973 13 Titles

BOOM, BOOM BABY, BOOM

BORN IN 1951? WHAT ELSE HAPPENED?

Wickham, NSW, Australia
Web: www.boombooks.biz
Email: email@boombooks.biz

Creator: Williams, Ron, 1934- author
Title: Born in 1951? : what else happened? / Ron Williams.
ISBN: 9780994601513 (paperback)
Series: Born in series, book 13.
Australia--History--Miscellanea--20th century.

Cover image: National Archives of Australia.
A4954, 1299/2 Photo L13044, Prime Minister Robert Menzies;
A1200, L13723, shearing;
A1200, L14292, Pioneer bus outside Parliament House;
Mitchell Library, hood_26479r, national service recruits.

TABLE OF CONTENTS

IMPORTANT FACTS AND FIGURES

George VI	King of England
Prime Minister of Oz	Bob Menzies
Leader of Opposition	Doc Evatt
Governor General	Sir William McKell
The Pope	Pius XII
US President	Harry Truman
PM of Britain (Until October)	Clement Attlee
PM of Britain (after October)	Winston Churchill

HOLDER OF THE ASHES:

1948	Australia 4 - 0
1950-1	Australia 4 - 1
1953	England 1 - 0

MELBOURNE CUP WINNERS:

1950	Comic Court
1951	Delta
1952	Dalray

ACADEMY AWARDS, 1951:

Best Actor   Humphrey Bogart (African Queen)
Best Actress Vivien Leigh (Streetcar named Desire)
Best Film   An American in Paris

INTRODUCTION TO THIS SERIES

This **book** is the 13th in **a series** of books that I have researched and written. It tells a story about a number of important or newsworthy Australia-centric events that happened in 1951. The **series** covers each of the years from 1939 to 1973, for a total of 35 books.

I developed my interest in writing these books a few years ago at a time when my children entered their teens. My own teens started in 1947, and I started trying to remember what had happened to me then. I thought of the big events first, like Saturday afternoon at the pictures, and cricket in the back yard, and the wonderful fun of going to Maitland on the train for school each day. Then I recalled some of the not-so-good things. I was an altar boy, and that meant three or four Masses a week. I might have thought I loved God at that stage, but I really hated his Masses. And the schoolboy bullies, like Greg Favvell, and the hapless Freddie Ebans. Yet, to compensate for these, there was always the beautiful, black headed, blue-sailor-suited June Brown, who I was allowed to worship from a distance.

I also thought about my parents. Most of the major events that I lived through came to mind readily. But after that, I realised that I really knew very little about these parents of mine. They had been born about the start of the Twentieth Century, and they died in 1970 and 1980. For their last 20 years, I was old enough to speak with a bit of sense. I could have talked to them a lot about their lives. I could have found out about the times they lived in. But I did not. I know almost nothing about them really. Their courtship? Working in the pits? The Lock-out in the Depression?

Losing their second child? Being dusted as a miner? The shootings at Rothbury? My uncles killed in the War? There were hundreds, thousands of questions that I would now like to ask them. But, alas, I can't. It's too late.

Thus, prompted by my guilt, I resolved to write these books. They describe happenings that affected people, real people. In **1951**, there is some coverage of international affairs, but a lot more on social events within Australia. This book, and the whole series is, to coin a modern phrase, designed to push the reader's buttons, to make you remember and wonder at things forgotten. The books might just let nostalgia see the light of day, so that oldies and youngies will talk about the past and re-discover a heritage otherwise forgotten. Hopefully, they will spark discussions between generations, and foster the asking and the answering of questions that should not remain unanswered.

The sources of my material. I was born in 1934, so that I can remember well a great deal of what went on around me from 1939 onwards. But of course, the bulk of this book's material came from research. That meant that I spent many hours in front of a computer reading electronic versions of newspapers, magazines, Hansard, Ministers' Press releases and the like. My task was to sift out, **day-by-day**, those stories and events that would be of interest to the most readers. Then I supplemented these with materials from books, broadcasts, memoirs, biographies, government reports and statistics. And I talked to old-timers, one-on-one, and in organised groups, and to Baby Boomers about their recollections. People with stories to tell came out of the woodwork, and talked no end about the tragic, and funny, and commonplace events that have helped shaped their lives.

The presentation of each book. For each year covered, the end result is a collection of short Chapters on many of the topics that concerned ordinary people in that year. I think I have covered most of the major issues that people then were interested in. On the other hand, in some cases I have dwelt a little on minor frivolous matters, perhaps to the detriment of more sober considerations. Still, in the long run, this makes the book more readable, and hopefully it will convey adequately the spirit of the times.

Each of the books is mainly Sydney based, but I have been **deliberately national in outlook**, so that readers elsewhere will feel comfortable that I am talking about matters that affected them personally. After all, housing shortages and strikes and juvenile delinquency involved **all** Australians, and other issues, such as problems overseas, had no **State** component in them. Overall, I expect I can make you wonder, remember, rage and giggle equally, no matter where you hail from.

INTRODUCTION TO 1951

From the very first day, 1951 looked as if it would be a good year. All the early signs were positive. The economy was in great shape, with boom prices being paid for many of our primary products, especially record-breaking wool. Everyone who wanted a job had one, and working conditions, which had suffered during the War, were improving, granted at a slow pace. The population was booming both from natural increase, and from the huge numbers of European migrants who were being offered very good deals to settle here for three years. Steak was on the menu in most houses whenever they wanted it, beer was **often** available, and Christmas last year had been the best it had been for twelve years at least. All the hated rationing from the past had now gone, and the black markets had gone with it. Even the dreaded rabbits were on the decline, thanks to the new virus, myxomatosis, which was being successfully spread by mosquitoes down on the Murray.

Of course, there were a few flies threatening the ointment. Wages were fairly good, and so inflation was on the increase. Many people said that inflation was taking away **all** benefits, but, in truth, real standards of living were gradually increasing. The population boom was putting a great strain on housing, which had never recovered from the War, but bank loans were available with a big enough deposit, so that young couples were slowly getting their own place to live. Then again, there were more than enough strikes for everyone. It seemed that the whole population was always going on strike, and even worse, such strikes were never justified, except of course for one's own.

But these complaints were by-the-by. In all, things were pretty good for most people, so that I suggest the scene is set for you to have a very good and prosperous year. Let's see what happens.

Two background matters from 1950. Reds in Australia. Bob Menzies had come to power just over a year ago, and he lived up to his election promise that he would try to curb the power of the local Communist Party. This Party had gained control of most of the major Trade Unions in the nation, and was constantly calling on its members to strike. Menzies thought he could put an end to this, and he introduced a Bill that would have outlawed the Communist Party, and would also have taken all of their property. Further, he would have had the power to "declare" a person or organisation who was a Communist and who presented some sort of menace to the nation. It was clear that **persons who advocated a strike** would be seen as such menaces, so this Bill was seen in many quarters as denying the worker the right to strike. The Labor Party had not wanted to oppose the Bill outright, because, in the grubby world of politics, **they would have been seen as fellow-travellers**, so they stalled it for six months. But Menzies had got it through Parliament at the end of 1950.

The Communist Party and nine Unions promptly challenged the Act in the High Court, and the hearing had lasted till the Court's Christmas break. As yet, of course, there had been no prosecutions under the Act.

At the end of January, the nation was waiting for the High Court's decision. If the decision went against the Government, that is if the Court found the Act invalid, there was no expectation in anyone's mind that Menzies would back off. He knew his anti-Red strategy was a political winner, and he would undoubtedly join the attack again. The only unknown was **how** he would re-enter the fray.

Reds in Korea. For the last six months, the two great ideologies of the worlds, Capitalism and Communism, had been locked in a war in Korea. No one cares about how it started, because it was in all respects just a battle, between these two ideologies, that happened to be fought in a convenient foreign land. Each side wanted to say to the world, at last, that **it** was the most powerful, and that **it** was also the greatest champion of justice. And, the corollary was, that all other nations should adopt the political and economic system of the good guy.

So, by January 1951 the North Koreans, now supported by the Chinese, had pushed past the border to South Korea at the 38th Parallel, and were half way down the Korean peninsular. Then the South Koreans, now supported by America, and Australia, and by a few countries of the UN, had moved the front line right up to the Korean border with China. After that, they had all moved back South again, and were fighting just south of the border.

Throughout the month of January, and also through the month of February, the front lines did not move far. This might have been because there were various levels of talks going on in the UN to stop the war, but it was also because of the extremely cold weather the country suffered in winter. In any case, after all those months, both sides were back where they started from. America has lost about 4,000 sons killed, and 6,000 missing on the battle fields. Australia had lost over 100 dead, and 200 missing. The number of Reds killed would be about 2 billion, if you believed our propaganda machine. No one ever counts how many civilians were killed.

This issue, though, had not gone away. Unfortunately it will surface again and again, and we will catch up with it in later months.

A FEW BACKGROUND ISSUES

I mentioned strikes earlier, and I want to expand on these, because they will be with us every day of the year as you read this book.

While Australia was at war, the workforce had accepted work conditions that it would have rejected while we were at peace. This was because the picture could be painted, and often was, that if workers went on strike for better conditions, then our men fighting overseas would be put at risk. The work output from coal miners and wharfies, for example, could easily be directly linked to the war effort, so it made it much harder for them to maintain the rage of a major strike.

Work conditions suffered during the War. When it was over, the Unions wanted conditions restored now there was no impediment to striking. This they started to do on a grand scale, and **they got better at it by 1951**.

So every household was anxiously starting every day wondering if the trains would run, or the postman come. Would it have electricity or gas, and would the man bring the bread or ice or meat? If there was a strike, would notice be given, or would it be a lightning strike? Would Dad get to the office and find that there would be no trains to take him home? If one Union went on strike, would other Unions come out in sympathy?

Matters such as these were always in the minds of citizens. I will not lay much stress on them as I write this tome, but I ask you too to keep them in the back of **your** mind as you read along.

MY RULES IN WRITING THESE BOOKS

NOTE. Throughout this book, I rely a lot on reproducing **Letters** from the newspapers. Whenever I do this, I put the text in a different font, and indent it a little, and make the font somewhat smaller. **I do not edit the text at all.** That is, I do not correct spelling or grammar. If the text gets at all garbled, I do not change it. It's just as it was seen in the Papers of the day.

SECOND NOTE. The material for this book, when it comes from newspapers, is reported as it was seen at the time. **If** the benefit of hindsight over the years changes things, then I **might** record that in my **Comments.** The info reported thus reflects matters **as they were seen in and about 1951.**

THIRD NOTE. Let me also apologise in advance to anyone I might offend. In a work such as this, it is certain some people will think I got some things wrong. I am sure that I did, but please remember, all of this is **only my opinion.** And really, **my opinion does not matter one little bit in the scheme of things. I hope you will say "silly old bugger", and shrug your shoulders and keep reading on.**

FOURTH NOTE. Let me remind you that the writers of Letters to the newspapers did so with pen and ink. In the early years, this was really laborious, with **a pen and nib, and ink-well, and a blotter.** Over the next thirty years, fountain pens became popular and then some early ball-points came on the scene. Whenever they wrote, it was quite a task, and the fact that **they wrote so many Letters testifies to their passion.**

JANUARY NEWS ITEMS

Our Prime Minister, **Robert Menzies, received a very high honour from the King**. He appointed him to the Order of the Companion of Honour. I am not qualified to speak on what that implies, but you can get some idea of how prestigious it is by the fact that **the Order is restricted to 65 members**, and only 30 of these have been made during the 13 years of the King's reign.

The year 1950 was very wet, especially in the east of the nation. One town on the far north coast of Queensland, **Tully**, had its fair share. In fact, it recorded **312 inches of rain.** In case you remember our old units of measure, that is **almost nine yards of rain**.

Boxing is a big sport in Australia at the moment. For example, the main bout at Sydney Stadium each week is **broadcast right round the nation, and SP bookies** lay millions of Pounds in bets. Fans here are wanting more international bouts for our young men , and are calling for some overseas fighters to visit for a punch-up.

A big-name black fighter, Sugar Ray Robinson, would attract large crowds if he fought here. But there is a **regulation that says that visitors to Australia can take only 1,000 Pounds out of Australia**. Sugar Ray would want much more than that, so it looks like he will not come….

This applies to **all visitors.** We will miss out on **anyone who would want to be paid more than a grand**.

The winter in Korea is extremely cold. That means that **soldiers there need protective clothing, like wool.**

Given that the war there is ongoing, **wool sales in Australia are booming.** On January 12th, fine quality wool sold for 302 pence a Pound. This is well above **the golden dream of a Pound a pound.**

A couple in Victoria produced a set of quads. The Federal Government said it would give them **four Pounds a week for five years** to help with expenses. Then, one of the quads died. The question was what the allowance should be. If it stayed the same, would it not lead to **claims by parents of triplets for the same amount?** That would be hard on the budget, and was never intended. **What would you have done?....**

The Feds decided that the sum of four Pounds would stand, but that **the period would be reduced to one year. Which seems a reasonable way out for them.**

For cricket lovers. It was announced that the touring English cricket team will play a State match against Tasmania, but **it would not be broadcast.** This reminded me that **cricket was widely broadcast by ABC radio.** That included not just the Test matches, and not just the international matches against the Poms, **but also all Sheffield Shield matches....**

Ball-by-ball descriptions of South Australia playing Queensland **would occupy the radio for days on end.** This **annoyed lots of housewives,** but to a hopeful Test star like myself, it seemed that this was **the purpose that radios were invented for....**

A nostalgia moment. The Shield is now forgotten. Pity.

50th JUBILEE CELEBRATIONS

On January 1st, 1901, the collection of six States that had hitherto occupied this country were formally accepted as a nation. Fifty years later, it was time to celebrate this blessed occasion, so that various events were planned to be spread across 1951.

The first of these was the re-enactment of the Sturt expedition that had gone 1000 miles down the Murray River looking for the Inland Sea. To duplicate this trek, on January 1st, a number of people descended on Yass, in Central South NSW.

In fact the numbers doing the descending were fairly large. There were 22 civilians, and 29 Army officers carried in four three-ton trucks, a jeep, a bus, a utility, a trailer, three vans, and a car, all from Sydney. They picked up a 27-foot whale boat which had arrived by train in Yass the day before.

In addition to the official party, there were staff from the ABC radio, which covered the whole adventure, and film crews from the Commonwealth Film Unit.

Six officers and two actors were scheduled to row the whale-boat 35 miles per day, until it reached Goolwa in South Australia about February 11. One of the actors was Rod Taylor, who later became something of a Hollywood heart-throb.

The party was greeted in the streets of Yass, and autographs were asked for. Mr Anthony Sturt, the explorer's great grandson, was asked by a little girl if she could kiss his cheek, and he obliged. That night, they all attended a civic welcome. The next day they paraded through the streets of Yass in period costume, before they left for Gundagai. When the party reached Yass, soldiers quickly put up 12 tents for camping in, and army cooks prepared an evening meal for all. There were no Aboriginal men there to welcome them, because all of them were down at the riverbank with spears and wearing paint to make the film "more authentic."

Comment. If you think that conditions would not be as hard as on the original trip, you would be correct. The only input required from the magnificent eight was rowing downstream. Mind you, doing that for 1,000 miles was no easy task, but in fact they reached Goolwa exactly on time.

POWER SHORTAGES

One consequence of many strikes in the mines, power stations, and railways, was that the ordinary householder in all our cities was always uncertain whether there would be enough electric power for their normal daily tasks. Not surprisingly, this irked them.

Letters, P James. In our area, we are having power interruptions on an average of three to four hours.

It would be much more preferable, it seems to me, for power to be withheld for, say, two days a week **from businesses**, with the assurance that for the rest of the week, power would be available. Given 24 hours notice that power would not be available on the following day, staff could be advised, and the financial burden more equitably apportioned as between employer and employed, and production could be planned with some degree of confidence.

Letters, PAST CURSING. It seems clear that our power troubles can be resolved at once, first by staggering working days and using all seven days to the week, and secondly, by mobilising and getting into continuous use, with appropriate subsidies to the owners, every piece of emergency equipment, however small, in much the same way that the mosquito fleet saved the British army at Dunkirk.

There was no compulsion in that operation. The call went out from a leader, and everything that would float set out across the Channel and did the job. If we had a leader, we could have our power Dunkirk tomorrow. But alas....

Letters, HOUSEHOLDER. I have received a circular from the local council, probably like many others, requesting that as a householder and resident, I should assist in **the Jubilee celebrations by illuminating my home on January 29th**.

For the past week, we have been deprived of all electricity and light for varying periods both day and night. One would not object to illuminations under normal circumstances, but the plan is out of place and ironical in the present intolerable circumstances.

THE MINERS' STRIKE OF 1951

In the coal industry, the principal arbitrator of disputes between miners on the one hand, and management and owners on the other, was the Coal Industry Tribunal, Mr Justice Gallagher. Just before the miners' three-week Christmas holiday began, he awarded the miners **an incentive of an eleventh day's pay, if they had previously worked ten consecutive days in that fortnight.**

The miners did not like this type of incentive. They were interested first and foremost in not being killed in the pits. None of them wanted to be brought home dead by a horse and dray. They reasoned (with good cause) that management would be asking them to work in unsafe conditions towards the end of each fortnight. After the holidays, they rejected the deal, and the Miners Federation indicated, in their normal belligerent fashion, that they were **considering** the proposition that all mines would work only four days each week instead of the normal five. This arrangement would continue until the Tribunal came to his senses, and gave them a cash increase instead.

The State Government, sensing that here was a great opportunity to gain public support by squashing the miners, then "announced some of the most drastic fuel cuts ever applied." The idea was that if they caused enough discomfort to everyone, they could say that the miners were responsible, and end up breaking the strike, and thus have a landmark victory over the Communist-led miners.

For industry, the new restrictions meant that no shop, office, warehouse, restaurant, hotel, or theatre in Sydney or Newcastle could use electricity, starting midnight Thursday. It also meant that electricity would be cut off from all industries for next Tuesday and Wednesday. **In the home,** usage of electricity for making meals was restricted to three nominated times, of an hour and a half, each day. The number of lights allowed was a maximum of two 40-watt bulbs. No power could be used for radiators, electric washing machines, hot-water systems, and electric irons.

Along with these broad statements were a host of supporting details. To give you an idea of this, so that you can appreciate that **the whole ambush was well planned,** and not a spur of the moment job, I enclose a small fraction of the new regulations.

There will be no exemption for factories producing liquor, aerated waters, soft drinks, fruit essences, cordials and syrups, fruit juices, flavouring essences, malted milk, malt extract, confectionery, chocolate, ice cream, flavoured ices, ice blocks, custard powder, jelly crystals, fruit jellies, jams, conserves, vinegar, pickles, spices, sauces, condiments, cornflower, macaroni, vermicelli, castor sugar, icing sugar, cakes, pastries, biscuits, processed breakfast food or the like.

Arthur Fadden, the Acting Prime Minister, flew to Sydney for meetings with the Joint Coal Board, Mr Justice Gallagher, and State Ministers. He weighed in with the threat that if the strikes went ahead, then the three miners' leaders would be prosecuted for contempt of Court. Gallagher also promised similar action, so all sides were now poised for a serious dispute after the long weekend.

On the Tuesday, the restrictions were applied fully. There was much muttering in the Press that this was a put-up job, and that coal was no shorter in supply than it always was, and that there was adequate supply to last for months even if miners worked to a four-day programme. **Then, on that Tuesday night, on the instructions of the NSW Premier McGirr, all restrictions were lifted.** He gave no reason whatsoever. He just issued instructions that they were off, and that people could have their early morning cup of tea again.

On the next day, January 31st, the Miners' Union met to decide whether they would call for a reduction in the working week. They had, in fact, so far only suggested that they might do so, and left the matter open for decision. But now, after the back-down by the State Government, it seemed that they would most probably let cooler heads prevail, and go back to the negotiating table. This would have been about the industry norm, and if they had done so, this little spat would have passed unnoticed, except for the egg stuck firmly to the faces of some State Ministers.

By now, you will have gathered that there are still some legs to this story. Indeed, you are right, and I will return to it in February.

SUNDAY SPORT

The idea that sport could be played on a Sunday was not fully accepted by the Churches. Sunday, to them, was a day of rest, a day for the family, and sometimes of contemplation, and of church-going. So, perhaps it was alright to fit in a game of some sort, but only if it was played in a reverential manner.

Beyond that, the new idea that sport should be organised, and that big grounds be opened to them, and that people should pay to enter, was anathema to them.

Letters, Bishop W Hilliard, Rev S McKibben. No doubt the Chief Secretary's action in granting permission to the LTAA to play championship tennis at White City yesterday, and to charge admission, has pleased a large section of the community.

By another large section, however, it is deeply deplored, and that for at least three reasons.

Firstly. It will be regretted that the LTAA has now apparently joined the company of those who disregard the sanctity of Sunday, and set up a false antithesis between religion and organised sport, forcing so many of our young folk to choose between them, when they are enthusiastically devoted to both. This cannot be good for sport in the long run.

Secondly. It marks another step in the community's decline towards the **full-orbed** Continental Sunday which, we are convinced, and many observers agree, would be a calamity for the bulk of our people, as well as dishonouring God.

Thirdly. The granting of similar permissions in other cases of recent date, added to this, creates a feeling of uneasiness concerning the general policy of the present Chief Secretary, at a time when such determined attacks are being made on the sacred character of Sunday by financially interested pressure groups.

In our judgement, there is a special responsibility upon those temporarily invested with discretionary authority in the administrative sphere, to scrutinise with the utmost care any proposals that may affect the moral and spiritual sanctities upon which the ordered life of the community rests.

Letters, F Finlayson, Silverwater Speedboat Club. The LTAA would be well advised to open its gates on Sundays, but earmark profits for some charitable cause.

Letters, R Langdon. Mr Clive Evatt, or the McGirr Government, has no mandate from the people to destroy the sacredness of Sunday and to install in its place the Continental-type Sunday, which it is now proved, was but a prelude to Continental Communism.

Letters, G Goodsell. If young Australians want to play championship tennis on Sundays, and the people want to watch, why shouldn't they?

I have never been to such a dreary and uninteresting place as Sydney on a Sunday, yet I would hesitate to state that we are of better moral fibre than the Europeans.

Letters, ONE OF THE SINNERS. Can it be that some 400 million European sinners dishonour their creator each Sunday, while the chosen Australian people alone know how to follow His laws in this matter.

Letters, F Wilson. Mr Goodsell may find Sydney a dreary and uninteresting place on a Sunday, but those who follow Christ do not.

He will be a happy man if in due time he realises that the welfare of the soul is of much greater importance than the pleasures of the senses.

Letters, C King, Secretary, Lord's Day Observance Society, Taree. The public are entitled to know that the same relaxation on Sunday sport was allowed in England several years ago, and the charities were to receive handsome dividends. But we find today that the producers receive 50 per cent of the fees, while the charities receive a very small fraction.

Your readers may be sympathetically disposed to Mr Evatt's policy, but revise their opinions when they realise that, at some future date, commercialisers will exploit the workers' rest for the own selfish ends.

Letters, John Mather. I do not agree with the idea that the Continental type Sunday was but a prelude to Continental Communism.

If that were so, then the US, with their fully commercialised and therefore presumably quite un-sacred Sunday, would long ago have become a Communist country.

DIFFERENT ATTITUDES TO CRICKET

In the days before TV, cricket lovers were well catered for with by ball-by-ball broadcasts of most major matches on

ABC radio. This made **them** smile, but there were no grins on **faces that liked music and commentary** on their ABC. But there were other points to be taken into consideration.

Letters, S Evans. The two Test matches concluded, although resulting in victories, have surely made Australian cricket lovers realise how much our world supremacy in cricket rested on Bradman.

Our present team will be a pushover for the powerful West Indies team next year, unless drastic action is taken to remove the alarming weaknesses that have crept into our batting strength.

Hassett is a shrewd and resourceful captain, but is no substitute for the Napoleon of cricket, who, at the age of 42, should have seven years of cricket in him yet.

I suggest that our Board of Control should prevail on Sir Donald Bradman to return to the game forthwith, not only to take over the captaincy and impart strength and resolution to our batting, but also for the great stimulus to the morale of the team his very presence always provided.

Letters, A Neyroud. One almost courts death by violence if one complains about this daily mumbling commentary on the Test Matches.

In the streets, in factories, and in the bush, one has to suffer this tedious mumbo-jumbo-jargon punctuated by hysterical outbursts when something supposedly "extraordinary" happens.

There is no escape, for, apart from the radio and the newspapers, the Test is the sole topic of conversation. It is taken for granted that everybody, without exception, treats these cricket games as a matter of vital concern.

It is indeed unfortunate that such persistent and enthusiastic publicity is not duplicated for greater production, recruiting, and preparedness in general.

NEWS AND VIEWS

Letters. A MINER, Cessnock Eagle. I would like to belt the living daylight out of the Editors of the Sydney daily papers. I write sensible, moderate letters to them, but they won't publish them because these letters **argue the case for some understanding of the miners.** Miners are quite reasonable and, if the papers wanted to, they could make them seem so. But they print any rubbish they can to make them look mean and foolish. I would like to do a few mean and foolish things to these editors.

News Item, withdrawals from the dollar pool. The Treasurer, Mr Fadden, indicated today that he would not relax Australia's dollar restraints so that a middleweight fight could take place. The promoters were planning a fight between Sugar Ray Robinson, the world Welterweight champion, and local Dave Sands, the Empire Lightweight champion. However, it was certain that Robinson's purse from the fight would exceed 1,000 Pounds, which is the maximum that any person can take from the country.

Mr Fadden indicated that Robinson would not be able to put the money into a bank here and take it out back to America.

Russian crabs. Letters, Delemere Usher. On occasion, protests have been voiced concerning the importation of Russian crab and similar luxuries, especially as some articles could be obtained from our Allies.

Next time a would-be purchaser orders that tin of crab, a moment's consideration should be given to the fact that it is caught, processed, and tinned by political prisoners sentenced to life imprisonment. Well may the gods laugh at the spectacle of democratic stomachs contentedly digesting the product of slave labour.

FEBRUARY NEWS ITEMS

The Brits and nationalisation. **People in Australia were uneasy about happenings in Britain** over nationalisation of the steel industry. There, the Labour Government is about to do that. Here, in Australia, one of the main issues of the 1949 federal election was nationalisation. Labor had been soundly defeated on this. Most people wanted it to go away permanently.

But the success of Britain's Labour Government is making some people think that **nationalisation might make a come-back here**. And, if that happens, maybe the coal industry would be next, and maybe then the wharfies. **Many people are getting nervous as the Brits get closer** and closer to their goal.

Just in case though that you do not remember, nationalisation did not revive in Australia, though **many old-style Labor politicians clung to the hope for years.**

Polio is on the increase round the nation. Deaths in Sydney year-to-date were 33 compared to 6 last year. **This was a disease that killed and maimed, and was dreaded by every parent.** At this time, there was no cure, and prevention was the main hope....

A visiting eminent scientist from Britain assured Australian audiences that **polio was not spread by the wind**, as was commonly believed in some quarters.

Whaleboat sailors. The Army officers who took part in the Sturt whaleboat expedition had another adventure in stall for them **in an Adelaide hotel**. All of them went to dinner, but one of them was wearing part of **his**

expedition uniform including the leggings he had made the journey in. He was refused entry.

The officers then left en masse. As they were departing, a message came through from the Army, ordering them to stay in the hotel. Feathers were unruffled, and the party returned to the dining room and were fed.

Flying saucers were back. Professor Cotton of Sydney University added his bit to the debate by saying that they were caused "by red corpuscles of blood as they passed over the retina of the eye." Several people were quick to ask if this explanation could cover mass sightings. Did everyone involved have active red corpuscles?

Young lads of 18 years of age will be called up to do their National Service in the Army or Navy in April. This service will involve a total of three months in camp, and then three years in the Citizens Military Forces on a part-time basis. This move was to prepare the nation for some sort of attack that our political masters were talking about. It was not yet envisaged the new recruits would be sent to fight in Korea.

The Sydney Morning Herald (SMH) is promising readers a spectacular parade of cartoon strips and jokes in its 18-page easy-to-read comic supplement in its Sunday version. It mentions Tarzan, Vic Flint, and The Saint. But to my mind, the Sunday Telegraph scooped the comics pool with Ginger Meggs, Dagwood, Li'L Abner, Prince Valiant, Mandrake, and Bib and Bub. It also had a section run by Charlie Chuckles that every child needed to live through.

THE COAL STRIKE 1951

At the end of last month, we suspected that the coal strike would go on. And indeed, it did. For the month of February, it broadened out on three fronts.

The first front. This was a relatively minor confrontation, spread over about a week, in NSW State Parliament, when the Opposition, led by Vernon Treatt, accused the Government of completely fabricating the coal crisis of the previous month.

The attack was led by fiery Clive Evatt. "Last week, we were told by the Joint Coal Board that, unless severe rationing was introduced, there would be a breakdown of essential services. This report was obviously false, and there should be an enquiry as to who the bureaucrats were that were responsible for it."

Opposition Leader Treatt said the shutdowns were evidence of Governmental "hypocrisy, double-talk, and incompetence. It is absolutely scandalous that people have been thrown out of employment and the whole life of this great city degraded because of Government blundering." One Member said the Government and the Joint Coal Board had together contrived the most serious and costly blunder in the State's history.

Of course, the McGirr Government had a majority in the Lower House so that no censure motion was brought against it. But the debate got a lot of attention, and it did serve to undermine the case for further future restrictions.

The **Letter** below reflects the mood of the public.

Letters, H.P.W. May I ask if someone in authority will inform the public how it is that power restrictions could be lifted last night, when only last Thursday they became effective, and it was then stated that coal supplies were almost exhausted.

The housewife and others would be very interested to learn on what days during this period miners have seen fit to produce adequate stocks of coal which enable the gas and electric light authorities now to lift the ban. Has "John Cit" once again been then victim of a colossal joke?

The second front. Arthur Fadden, the Federal Treasurer, kept getting involved, and he was good at issuing threats. He mentioned the dreaded Crimes Act a few times, but finally he settled on instructing the Federal Attorney General to bring charges against Idress Williams, Bill Parkinson, and George Grant, three Red miners' leaders, for contempt of Court.

The basis for this charge was that these three gentlemen had been jailed during the 1949 coal strike, and had given the Arbitration Court an assurance that they now saw the law of the land as taking precedence over Union rules, and that **they would not offend similarly in future**. On that basis, they were released. Now, it was claimed, they had led the strikers into similar industrial action, and **should be jailed as having broken their previous assurances**.

Dr Evatt, despite his leading position in the Federal **Labor** Party, undertook the defence of these three **Communists**. The court action took about ten days, and concluded with the decision that **the three men were not guilty**.

The third front. Meanwhile, what was happening to the strike? Well, there seemed to be a lot. Ministers and Governments, and Boards and Unions, and now the ACTU, were all getting very involved. The miners decided that they **would** go on strike, and for one day in each of the last three weeks in February, they did not turn out for work. This got the State Government quite cross and they reintroduced the restrictions that they had removed earlier. But by now, nobody thought that they were needed, especially when it was made known that the total coal production for those three weeks exceeded expectations made prior to the strikes. Still the restrictions, mainly on factories, were persisted with, on certain days, and there was also much talk, mainly silly talk, about **zoning** industry, along similar lines to the letter from Mr James in the previous Chapter. Nothing substantial came out of all this.

The ACTU was no help at all. It came in as the representative of most trade Unions, and while it was sympathetic to the miners themselves, it had mixed sympathies for the Communists who led them. Predictably, despite the big fanfare of its entry into the dispute, it soon fell out with the Reds among the miners' leaders, and retired a bit hurt.

So, by the end of the month of February, things were still unresolved. Everyone was in full battle dress, but the miners were working their four days, and increasing coal stocks. This was hurting **the State Government, because they now had a vested interest in stocks falling**. **It was a nice old mess.** The big question was whether the various actors could keep it going for another month, before they sat down and reached an agreement. On performance to date, it seemed likely that they could. But we will have to wait till next month to see.

THE EXECUTION OF JEAN LEE

On February 19th, a Sydney woman, Jean Lee, was executed in Melbourne for her part in the murder of a local bookmaker. She, and two men, had become acquainted with the bookie for the purpose of robbing him of his takings. They had gone with him to his dwelling, and after drinking a lot, had strangled him to death.

The evidence against the three was convincing, and after passing through the Courts in Australia, an appeal was made to Britain's Privy Council. This appeal failed, basically through lack of substance. Six days later the sentence was carried out.

The matter is famous because it was the last time that a woman was executed in Australia.

Letters, H Cranston. The hanging of three persons in Australia made many people consider whether this practice should be continued in this supposedly enlightened country.

There is no fundamental difference between the public destruction of criminals in the arenas of Rome, and this event in Victoria.

Up to comparatively recent time, capital punishment was carried out for a large number of crimes, but had little effect in preventing repetition of the offences. But as reform improved the economic and educational standards of the people, these crimes diminished. As poverty and insecurity are removed from any society, and are coupled with wider educational and cultural facilities, so violence and crime decrease.

But today the people are fed horror, violence, and sadism by the radio, cinema, magazines, comics, movies and the Press. In such an atmosphere, must we only blame those who commit violence, and exact a barbaric punishment? Or take some of the responsibility ourselves, for allowing this state of affairs to continue.

The lives of people, even criminals, should not be the plaything of politicians. Capital punishment should be abolished by Act of Parliament throughout Australia.

Comment. Before I started writing this book, I was aware of the Lee execution. I was certain that when I came to research it now, I would find that a great deal of public interest for and against the execution would be evident. I thought also that it would open up a lot of comment on the whole idea of capital punishment. In both of these, I was absolutely wrong.

In Melbourne, the trial and appeal had been widely reported, but not so the execution. What happened was that *The Age* Editorials did not mention it at all, and on the morning of her death, "a small crowd waited outside the gaol for a few hours after her death." The hangings were reported at the bottom of Page Three.

In Sydney, the *SMH* carried an editorial which mentioned the Lee case only in passing, and argued gently for retention of the death penalty in some special cases. It was really neither for nor against the Lee execution. When it came to Letters, instead of being inundated, at least on capital punishment, the only Letter published was the one above. The death was reported in only 14 column-inches on Page

Five in the *SMH*. There were no demonstrations reported in Sydney.

In all, the matter passed with so little comment that it surprised me. I think at times that it might have just been the Press, who for some reason of their own, decided to keep the matter as quiet as possible. But there is nothing else to support that theory, and I have to admit that I was wrong. I am still sitting here scratching my head.

IMMIGRATION OF GERMANS

Immigration of Germans en masse. In late February, a mention was made in Parliament of the idea that we should allow some 25,000 migrants Germans into this country. This raised the hackles of many people, and the correspondence was intense.

Letters, Kenneth McClean. I have returned from a visit to Germany to read that my own country is proposing to admit 25,000 Germans this year as migrants.

This is a shocking proposition. It must be challenged at once. The German has not changed. The youngest least of all. My few weeks there convinced me that the Nazi spirit is still very much alive, and that to talk of careful screening is utter nonsense.

I came across evidence of the manner in which these supposedly de-Nazified Germans hid their real thought. One Australian immigration official told me that he would mis-trust every German he interviewed, but that higher officialdom in Australia was pressing for migrants from that source.

I fervently pray that we will tell the Government that these people are not wanted here. There are thousands of better types waiting to come here from all parts of Europe and Britain.

Letters, G Reid. I have been a wheat farmer in Western Australia, and a sugar planter in Northern Australia. I have been through all the other States, and though my people have been Scottish for hundreds of years and there is certainly no German blood in my veins, I do not hesitate for a moment to say that the German settlers have always been among the best primary producers I have met. They are very industrious, honest, clean, and more thrifty than we are ourselves.

Letters, Ernest Jones. From my personal experience of German POW's, I would say that the average German is no different from the average Britisher, though perhaps a little more courteous and industrious.

Letters, Mijiran Sarkissian. Although my brother and I are of the same parentage, my brother is not me nor am I he. If he commits a murder that does not mean that I have or will commit a murder, too.

I admit that some Germans, perhaps many, did cruel and fiendish things during the two World Wars, but I would be inhuman, unchristian, and undemocratic to brand all Germans cruel and fiendish, just as I would be foolish to think of all Germans as Martin Luthers or Bachs because Luther and Bach were Germans.

Letters, A F Walter. Being a German who has lived here for 28 years, and not being a Jew, I have a lot of relatives living in Germany. With them I am in close contact and feel I am able to judge the prospective influence of German migration into Australia.

The screening of applicants by our men there is of little, if any, value. Among my relatives I have four nephews who were SS men. They are now under new names and no "screener" will be able to identify them.

All my relatives are still convinced that dictatorship is the only healthy political regime. They despise democracy and laugh at Parliament which they call a chatter booth.

As a German, I have often had, during the last two years, opportunity to function as an interpreter to New Australians speaking German. I spoke with about 20 German women married to Poles or other Slavs. Not even one of them was satisfied with what they have found here. When I asked them whether they would prefer to go back to Germany nearly all replied they would be glad to see the day they could. Many complaints were uttered in a hectic, hysterical way similar to the Goebbels line of propaganda.

We say rightly that we need many thousands of migrants to help defend our country, but is there one sane person who imagines that a single young German migrant would help to defend Australia?

German people as a whole are as honest, decent, and good as any other nation. There should be no prejudice against Germans. But the young generation is still intoxicated by the horrible propaganda machine of the Nazi Party. We will have to wait many more years until time will change the mind of those people.

Letters, G Wood, UK Ex-Services Association, Sydney. The members of this Association do not favour the mass migration of Germans to Australia.

We feel that the Government would be better advised to correct the disabilities imposed on British ex-Service migrants – thus securing more of them – than to flood the country with ex-enemy immigrants.

The crux of the matter is – can ex-enemy migrants be effectively screened? One of our members who lately served with the British Army of Occupation in Germany thinks it impossible. So do my "New Australian" friends. So do many knowledgeable people.

I cannot but feel that had Australia been effectively bombed, and its women and children machine-gunned, the question of German migration would not have arisen.

Letters, W S Kent Hughes, Federal Member. As the result of certain letters I have received during the past two months, I would be grateful if you would allow me to announce publicly that the views held by Miss Margaret Kent Hughes on any political matters, including German migration, have no connection whatsoever with any views held by myself.

No Australian desires to assist in the migration of large numbers of Nazis, but no fair-minded Australian will condemn a race on account of the excesses of a few. I wonder what Australians would say if America refused entry to all our citizens because some of our teachers and trade-union leaders are Communists.

Letters, (Miss) M Kent Hughes. In reply to Mr W S Kent Hughes, I wish to state clearly my views on the question of German migration.

I have never condemned, nor would any other sane person condemn, a whole race on account of the excesses of a few. As my brother surely knows, 12 million (some put the figure as high as 20 million) innocent people cannot, even with Nazi efficiency, be massacred by a few; even so, it has never been a question of condemning the whole German race.

I and others who are opposing this plan to bring 100,000 young Germans to this country in the next four years, do so because they will be the ones who received their whole education under Hitler – the disastrous effects of which I saw as early as 1936 and 1937 – and so would be a threat to our Australian democracy.

I wonder what Mr W S Kent Hughes's reaction would be if the proposal was to bring 100,000 Japanese here?

When a new generation has arisen in Germany, free from Hitlerism, then it will be time enough to re-open the question of German migration. To date, there has been no effective de-Nazification in Western Germany.

COUNTRY TRAIN TRAVEL

One of the many irritations that no one seemed to be doing anything about was country train travel. Letters kept piling into the Papers, full of complaints about the simplest journeys, but the only response was to cut more lines and more trains. Perhaps the official attitude was that if the services were cut to zero, there would be no complaints. I can see the logic in that, yet I feel there could have been another approach.

The Letter below is typical of many.

Letters, B Henry, Kempsey. The train journey from Kempsey to Sydney was a disgrace. The train leaving Kempsey consisted of old-type suburban carriages. By the time Taree was reached, people were standing, and by Maitland, there was hardly breathing room. We had to leave the train at Telahrah, and had to wait two hours for a transfer to Maitland. 200 people did this. We got out in the pouring rain and found our baggage waiting there for us on the kerb in the rain. The ongoing train was already half-full of passengers. The train left Maitland with many passengers who had already been in the train for ten hours standing.

At Sulphide Junction signal-box, the train was held up for half an hour while two divisions of the Newcastle Flyer passed it. From here on in, it became an all-station train, and at each station people struggled to get on or off an already crowded train.

A buffet car was on the train, but passengers could not reach it because of the congestion. An attendant forced her way along the corridor to charge hungry people nine pence for a small piece of fruit cake.

Why was this trainload of wet, hungry people not run as a through train from Broadmeadow?

THE FIRST FLYING SAUCERS

People round the world had seen many cartoons of flying saucers scooping up citizens from Earth, and taking them to other planets and experimenting with them. They had seen movies of little green monsters invading the earth, and only at the last minute was the President saved.

But now, these same people were looking out at night and seeing bright lights moving across the sky, and sometimes actually landing and perhaps leaving crop circles for us to wonder at. Most of these foreign objects were reported to authorities or to newspapers, yet every one of them was explained away. As time went on the authorities got very adroit at saying there was no substance to the sightings, but at this early stage there was no set line of patter.

The News Item below shows a weak attempt by a New York paper to make sense of the situation.

New York, Feb 14th. American newspapers today criticised the Government for not revealing the true nature of flying saucers earlier.

The boss of the Nuclear Physics Research Office, Dr Urner Liddell, said that the saucers were actually plastic balloons, sent up by the US Navy scientists. All reported sightings could be correlated with balloon releases.

For four years, spokesmen for the Government had told people that they were fanciful, irrational, and trouble-making when they reported sightings. The Air Force and National Guard and local police had all wasted a large sum of money because of the reports. There is a wide-spread call on the Navy and Government to explain themselves.

Comment. I wonder what those sightings were all about. In the long run, thousands were made by sensible people. **Yet no coherent explanation was ever given.**

NEWS AND VIEWS

News from Goolwa. Remember the voyage of the intrepid mariners down the Murray for the big celebration in January? Well, on February they made it to their destination at Goolwa, where they rowed their whale-boat safely to shore. They were right on time.

They were given a reception of British cheers by 5,000 people and a small fleet of pleasure craft and a large ferry. Each of the eight men was given a specially crafted medal, and they all attended a celebratory ceremony at a memorial erected to Sturt. The epic trip was over without a major incident.

New York, Press report. A band of Japanese soldiers at Anatahan **in the Marianas Islands are still fighting WWII.** Six years after the war was officially over, they have **refused to accept the defeat of Japan**, and attack anyone who comes near them. Japanese authorities are **enlisting the aid of family members** who will approach them to tell them of the true situation.

MARCH NEWS ITEMS

March 1ˢᵗ. This is a sad day for Australia, so I will be as brief as possible. The English cricket team has been out here for a few months, and has played many matches, four against Australia and a dozen against the various State sides. **In the Fifth and last Test, they had an eight-wicket win. This was their first win since the War….**

I can sum up the feelings of the Poms by telling of **a well-dressed English woman in the grandstand,** while down on the field the Pom players were celebrating with a crowd of spectators. This good lady was sitting there **crying quietly, all to herself.** When asked by a reporter if she was alright, she said "I certainly am. This is **the greatest day** in my 40 years of life. **Even when my husband came home from the War."**

Gamblers in Australia did not have many places where they could bet legally. There was no off-course betting on horses, no legal casinos, so no chance to play baccarat, pontoon, poker, two-up, even dominoes for a beer. So illegal betting flourished, and **the network of SP bookmakers spanned the nation….**

The police made sporadic raids on gambling groups at places like illegal casinos, and the back-yard of every pub in Australia. This was standard fare for punters, and in most casinos, the organisers regularly paid the fines of anyone who got caught.

150,000 migrants had come to Australia from the European mainland in the last three years. Most had signed **a contract to work in a particular job for two years.** Officials are now admitting that **thousands of migrants have left their defined jobs,** and cannot be traced. When they are traced, **they can be deported.** But so far, only 42 have suffered that fate.

Most European migrants are good citizens. Included in these was **an Italian who had been here for two months.** He had been working as a cleaner. He saw a 4-year-old girl struggling in deep water in a Sydney Bay, and dived in to help her. **He hit his head on a rock, and was killed....**

He was penniless, had no friends and no relatives. Thus he was destined **for a Pauper's Funeral.** Radio Station 2GB broadcast his plight, and public donations provided the money **for his decent burial.**

On March 26th, **all Sydney newspapers** announced in their columns that their price would **rise a penny,** up to four-pence. Privately they told their **newsagents** that **their** share would be **ten per cent of the increase.** This made the agents sad, because, for selling over the counter and for home deliveries, **they were now getting 25 per cent of the initial price.** They went on strike for about four days, but the newspapers **appointed new agents. The strike collapsed.** But **for those four days, there were no papers.** At that time, of **no internet, this caused a crisis** in many homes.

THE COAL STRIKE CONTINUED

A major breakthrough came when the Coal Industry Tribunal called the mine owners and the Unions **together** for a **compulsory** conference. Now, it might seem obvious to everyone that getting the warring parties together in the one room might be useful. But prior to this date, the mine-owners had a policy of refusing to meet face-to-face with the miners because it was their strategy not to do so while the latter were out on strike. This suicidal policy of some standing was finally thrown out the window, when Mr Justice Gallagher at last earned his keep, and called the parties together, under compulsion to attend.

As it turned out, **the two parties**, without the help of the State and Federal Government, and the ACTU, and the Joint Coal Board, and the newspapers, and hundreds of others, **actually made progress**. Both sides to the dispute were sick of it, and wanted it to end. The miners gave ground after a week and called off the next week's strike. They decided at the same time to call aggregate meetings of the miners to ask them to cancel the one-day strikes. They did this on condition that no further prosecutions would be launched against their leaders, and that the threatened use of the dreaded Crimes Act against them would not happen. It was also decided that the whole business of the incentives for a full fortnight's work would be put back to Gallagher for his decision, and that both sides would make submissions on what they wanted and why.

Comment. What a silly strike. Everyone was a loser. The miners and mine-owners came out of it in exactly the same position as they had started. The State and Federal

Governments had shown themselves to be a mob of opportunists, wanting to exploit the Red Menace, and just too disorganised to do so. The Tribunal was criticised for his tardiness in getting a solution, and the Joint Coal Board, a creation of the NSW Government, had done nothing, and had done it badly.

A more troublesome side to this pantomime was that, at the time, it was repeated over and over again, all across the nation. Granted, this was a severe example. But, on a smaller scale, this was happening everywhere. It has been argued that work conditions and wages did thus improve, and so it worked out in the long run. But it was very wasteful for the nation, and upsetting for the person in the street. It might be that a different system could have been worked out. That, however, did not happen. In fact, the system of confrontation lasted for decades, and despite elaborate mechanisms for reconciliation and arbitration, it would be an optimist who said that such confrontations were now a thing of the past.

THE RED BILL IN THE HIGH COURT

Robert Gordon Menzies always liked to travel overseas. He gloried in the limelight of overseas luminaries, and never turned away any opportunity for a good long trip. Last year, when it was obvious that he could not get his anti-Red Bill through the Senate, he had gone to England, America and Japan, leaving this obviously self-sufficient nation to survive without him for three months. Then when the New Year came, he went off to the Mediterranean and Britain for another two months, having a leisurely trip home by sea. But now, in March, here he was back again, raring to go.

And go he did. He spent the early weeks of March making it clear that he had power to call an election for both Houses of Parliament if the Labor Party continued to frustrate his proposed legislation. **Ho hum**, said some Labor members, because that message was getting stale. They had been hearing it now for nine months. He also emphasised another old message, one that said that a new war was getting close, and that we as a nation should start to worry about that. **Ho hum**, said the people, because that message too was now stale. It was quite obvious that, even with the sabre-rattlers in Korea, there was no likely threat of a major conflict in the near future.

But then, the High Court brought down its decision on the anti-Red Bill. **It threw it out of court**. Menzies, after a year of anticipation of prosecutions against the strike-prone Communists, was left without his major tool for breaking their Party. But he wanted to continue to flog the Red bogey. **What could he do?**

The Court brought down its decision on March 10. At about the same time, Labor signalled that it was about to block another Banking Bill that Menzies wanted passed. By March 16, Menzies had made up his mind that he had enough grounds to call for a double dissolution, and made his way out to Yarralumla to see Sir William McKell, the Governor General. McKell was an ex-Labor politician, so many Labor members supposed that he would not grant the Liberal Government the dissolution Menzies wanted. He thought about it for a day, and then agreed that elections should be held on April 28.

This was a nasty surprise to Labor. Not too long before, they had been thrown out of office, by a large majority, and had seen nothing happen since that would make the electors want them back. They had retained a majority in the Senate, but only because half of an old majority had been carried forward. This time, without any carry-forward at all, they could see no prospect of getting a majority in either House.

The Labor leaders were in a pretty bad state. Chifley had been sick for months, and though he was back in Parliament, there were many who thought he was not yet well enough. But he had not learned anything from his defeat, and **persisted in pushing socialism and nationalisation**. Arthur Calwell, never conspicuous for learning new lessons, was spending all his time yapping at the heels of the new Government Ministers, and harassing them on any little contradictions or slips he thought they made. "But you said **in 1942** that ….. and **now** you say…." That sort of thing.

Doc Evatt, on the one hand, agreed that the Commos were potentially a menace to the nation, **but** then rushed into Court to plead their case. He actually persisted with this approach right through to the Petrov affair in the early fifties. Even now, after the elections were called, he was censured by the Victorian Labor Party for defending the Reds in the recent miners' strike. His lack of judgement time and time again worked against him. So the Labor Party was doomed in these elections before they started.

The Liberals knew all of this, of course, and reacted with glee to the new push-over elections. Even Billy Hughes, nee William Morris Hughes, the Little Digger, said he would stand again. Given the fact that he had been in every Parliament since the beginning in 1901, and he was now 85 years of age, it might just be accepted as normal that he should run for office. But there had been speculation that he might stand down next time. Not likely. This time it would be too easy.

So both Parties suddenly found themselves selecting their own candidates, and getting ready for an election in six weeks. Things were not quite so **ho hum** now.

MacARTHUR MESSING UP IN KOREA

Winter persisted in Korea, and both the goodies and the baddies were reluctant to press past the 38th Parallel, and go into the other's territory. In Washington, there were all sorts of hawks calling for MacArthur to go North and invade. **Indeed, he himself was very keen to do this.** But, the doves won out and, for the time being, the battle-lines were preserved at where they stood.

But MacArthur, getting more erratic, distinguished himself towards the end of the month by suggesting, to the leader of the North Korean army, that **they** should meet near the current battlelines, **in a one-on-one situation**, and themselves seek to find a way of ending the war. This was a suggestion that he made without consulting the President or the Pentagon, and which simply amazed these gentlemen. Of course, they rejected the idea because they thought the conflict was not simply a war, but rather an expression of huge political differences, and that **the war was just**

an incidental expression of those differences. So, out of hand, MacArthur's plan was rejected by them, and at the same time, the North Korean military commander came back with a message that was quite scornful of the suggestion. He described it as mad, shameless, a bluff, and an insult to the Chinese people. Needless to say, the meeting did not take place, but doubts about the wisdom of MacArthur grew right across the world.

A LETTER FROM LEVITICUS

Occasionally it happened around 1951 that a seemingly capricious or irrelevant Letter grew legs, and others would follow and wander all over the place. Of course, this still happens at times now, but in those more leisurely days, such epoch-making Letters were much more common. Here is a good example, starting from a Letter that quoted Leviticus from the Old Testament, and which stirred many passions.

Letters, David Stead. Mr Arnold quotes Mosaic legend as a guide for distinguishing between poisonous and non-poisonous fish. This story has been responsible for the popular idea that scaleless fish are dangerous to eat, while fish with scales are safe.

But there is no such rule in nature. Many scaleless kinds are commonly eaten in various parts of the world, and are good food-fish. There are also the apparently scaleless, such as freshwater eels, which are classified by those following the Mosaic rule, as unclean. On the other hand, there are heavily scaled fish that are poisonous, such as parrot-fish, and castor-oil fish. So that the old rule of thumb is useless.

Quite a number of toad-fish or rabbit-fish are edible, and are regularly consumed as food in some parts.

Usually the skin is removed. With our little toad-fish, it is advisable to skin the fish before, say, serving to the cat. Sometimes, as I have found under a test, a cat will vomit after eating the whole fish, but not always. I have known humans to eat it without any disagreeable result, but I would not recommend it.

During the years I have had many amusing enquiries – mostly very serious, but none the less amusing – from people who yearned for eels, but whose spiritual advisers warned them of such "unclean" fish. They were all delighted when I told them that eels had microscopic scales deep-set in their skins.

Letters, Kerwin Macgrath. Australians are among the world's most fastidious fish eaters. How many of us still turn up our noses at a wholesome trevalli, being skinned and thrown into a frying pan, and run down the merit of commonplace but delectable leather-jacket? And, I ask, what is more delectable than fried shark and chipped potatoes.

Before the War, tunny was considered to be an inedible fish. I was in an angling party with Zane Gray, the famous cowboy author. We cooked some. As the Americans smacked their lips in satisfaction, the more discerning Australians stood aghast.

Who would eat bonita among us? But British sailors from carriers at Jervis Bay, relished this fish, fried or grilled. Australians are not only afraid of poisonous fish, but throw away most of what Zane Gray described as "the best, in quantity and quality, in the world."

Letters, Stan Kurrle. Mr Stead forgets that:

One. Moses was legislating for one small racial group which was to occupy an area of only 10,000 square miles. Moses did not have in mind Gentile Australians or Australian marine life.

Two. In that area, there were 250 miles of coast line. It is most probable that the examples given by Mr Stead did not exist in those few miles of water.

Three. Moses never claimed to be a marine biologist. To him, most scale fish were poisonous. It would be safer to assume all were, particularly if one would have to search for microscopic layers of scales to be certain.

Letters, P Holdsworth. The eleventh chapter of Leviticus does act as a guide to edible food. It does offer a guide to our high-priced meat, but whether the locust and the bald-locust and grass-hoppers would appeal to the discriminating palate is somewhat doubtful.

I notice that rabbits and bacon are taboo, and presumably oysters, as they have no feet, and lobsters, which have more than four feet, and are an abomination. This writer candidly confesses to a liking for both.

Letters, W Noble. An apparently scaleless fish not so far mentioned is the indigenous fresh water catfish of our western streams, which frequents the quieter waters of warrumboos or billabongs – a totally distinct type from all the unworthy salt water species.

It has an eel-like skin, attains an average weight of seven pounds, and is good sport with a rod and line. Its flesh is firm and white, has only a main backbone, and is splendid eating.

During recent times, specimens from the 'Bidgee have been propagated in the waters of our catchment area, and mature fish may now be found in the Cowpasture River about Camden, or lower down in the Nepean section.

The first two I caught were landed in the Narran River at New Angledool, 53 years ago, where King Combo, big chief of the Noongaburrah tribe, told me they called them "Tucki" ("plenty good fehella tucker").

He warned me of the sharp pines protruding from each end of the two gills, and the back fin behind the head. These spines are extremely dangerous, sometimes having caused death. Nevertheless, the flesh is not dangerous to eat. Along with Murray cod and yellow-belly perch, these catfish are looked upon as a great delicacy by the aborigines.

Letters, Russell Jones. For some years, I have tried to keep God's food laws, with great benefit to my health. Your various Letters miss the essential point. These laws were ordained by God as a guarantee against sickness if the Israel nations obeyed them. They were not, as some writers suggest, a "theory" of Moses, now debunked. Moses was only the intermediary.

Surely confession to a liking for food prohibited by God does not justify disregarding the Divine guidance, any more than in the case of adultery.

STUMPS DRAWN ON A CRICKET TOUR

The English cricket team had toured Australia since last November, and had convincingly lost all major games, including four Test matches. Then, surprisingly, in the last and Fifth Test, they won it.

At the end of every Test, there is always a scramble by the players to collect the stumps and bails to keep as souvenirs. By some unwritten convention, these goodies are generally shared out among the players, so that anyone who did well in that Test gets something, but in the long run everyone ends up about equal.

But not this Test. Here was cricket history in the making. England was about to win a Test. No... No.... Surely not. But in fact, Yes.... Yes ..... Jolly Good and Whatto. That meant that the stumps were of much more significance than normal, and so the usual conventions of a fair share went by the board. Thus, at the very end, when the players thought that the last run had been hit, stumps were uprooted by a mad scramble to take possession. But, alas, the ball was fielded, and so the stumps had to be replaced. Then this happened a second time. Then it happened a third time. But, at last, the Poms summed up their last bit of energy, and hit a real single, and the game was over. Then the final scramble occurred.

Compton, Lindwall, and Ian Johnson made a clean get-away with three stumps between them. Tallon, Miller and Morris were locked for minutes in a snatch-as-snatch can battle for the spoils of war.

It was a grand finish to a good tour, and showed that cricket was such a good way to produce good Empire relations.

NEW COMMONWEALTH SCHOLARSHIPS.

Menzies was now aware that during the War, and in the five years after the War, educational standards in Australia had progressively lagged behind the rest of the Western world. He sought to rectify this by introducing Commonwealth Scholarships so that a few thousand young people each year could reap the benefits of a tertiary education in any University faculty they were qualified for.

The scheme started in 1951, and paid all University fees, and provided a living allowance to those who were poor enough. The student accumulated no debt to the Commonwealth over the years so that, at graduation, he had nothing to pay back. This was a generous scheme that suddenly took the Universities out of the old-world torpor where they had been languishing, and pushed them towards a culture where red-blooded philistines gradually challenged the stuffiness and elitism that they had previously excelled at.

Personal comment. I can't help but think how lucky I was. I went off to Sydney University in 1952, with a Commonwealth Scholarship. I got paid a miserable allowance, but with the money I earned in holidays, I lived as well as I needed. I paid no fees, and at the end, importantly, I had no debt to anyone, and I was not bonded to work for any period. The whole operation was no strings attached, and left me free to be a full-time student.

I contrast it with the situation now. The fact that there is no living allowance means most young people need to work part time. This means they do not have the long, relaxed hours on campus when much of the true learning happened. It means too that they have to find the university fees, from their parents or somewhere like a loan, and hand them over each year. And it means they will have an average debt of about $20,000 dollars at their graduation. There is simply no comparison.

PERON HAS THE BOMB?

Buenos Aires, Argentina. News Item, March 25th. President Peron announced last night that his scientists have produced atomic energy by a startling new method, bypassing the usual processes and not using any uranium. He said that "the energy was produced by the same thermo-nuclear processes that occur naturally in the sun. To produce such reactions, enormous temperatures are needed – millions of degrees – and we have now managed that. We had our first tests on February 2nd, and achieved a controlled release of atomic energy. All problems in our trials have been exhaustively studied and overcome." He added that this was not a copy of what had been done elsewhere and that it was a far superior technique to that used by the US.

The world was startled and cautiously impressed. It was known that many German scientists had fled to Argentina during the War, and it was **possible** that they had provided the breakthrough. It was also just possible that Peron was inventing the story to impress his South American colleagues who he was just about to join in a Latin American conference. But there was no doubt in anyone's mind that if what he said was true, the whole pattern of international relations would change immediately.

Overnight, scepticism spread urgently. Scientists around the world were quick to doubt Peron, and scientific comments, in a few hours, changed from "much exaggerated" to "plain crazy." Peron was kind enough to make a second statement about the new toy, and added pointedly "I never tell a lie", which was a bit silly, because everyone knew he was a liar and much worse. Then his chief scientist, Dr Ronald Richter, said that the explosion was noiseless, generated more energy that an exploding star, and produced little radioactivity. Such a contradiction of the fundamentals of atomic energy brought howls of protest from round the world.

The following day it was all over. A new dominant player had **not** entered world politics, and no one had a new and superior weapon. It turned out, said Dr Richter, that in fact the "explosion" had only been on a test-tube model, and most of the details had been lifted from a theoretical paper by British scientist Sir John Cockcroft in the *Bulletin of*

Atomic Scientists. So the whole matter was a complete fraud, and did nothing to enhance the standing of the Argentine President in the very volatile world of South American politics.

Peron held the Presidency from 1946 to 1955, and again from 1973 to 1974. His wife Eva is remembered in the musical *"Evita"*, and the song *"Don't Cry for Me, Argentina."*

NEWS AND VIEWS

Letters, A Parsons. I have repeatedly advocated that a Government stud should be set up to breed our working dogs. How to get suitable people to run such a stud is hard.

I cannot agree with the statement that "one good thing the backyarders did, for both Kelpies and blues, was to keep the standard up to type". The type of Kelpie seen on exhibition at the Royal Easter Show does not conform to the standards of the true working Kelpie.

The truth is that the purebred working Kelpie sheep dog is possibly a dying breed today. Fifty years ago, 60 or 70 beautiful Kelpies could be seen working at the Sydney sheep-dog trials. To-day we are lucky if half a dozen Kelpies compete in the event.

Some graziers will pay good prices for the genuine article, but there are many country men who would not think of paying more than five Pounds for a pup, no matter how well bred. If a breeder cannot obtain decent prices there is just not much incentive to breed animals at all.

However, one of the main reasons for the degeneration in the breeds is that it impossible to obtain imported stock to refresh the existing bloodlines. It is tragic that so little assistance has been given to the breeders of the greatest breeds of working dogs that the world will ever know.

Letters, Ben Doig, Sane Democracy League. Now that the Reds have been given a temporary freedom, they are extending their activities. Parents should be warned that when teenagers are invited, during the next few weeks, to a "social evening" at the home of a little-known neighbour, it is most likely that the neighbour will be running a "cottage" lecture for Communist training and indoctrination.

The danger is greatest in industrial suburbs, but exists in all suburbs. When I lived in Gordon, I received an invitation to such a meeting in Killara; the bait used was classical music.

Letters, R Wilson, North Sydney. Bandicoots are everywhere on the North Shore. They are digging up all the vegetable patches in back yards, and the flower beds in front yards. They are covered in fleas, which are infecting our cats and dogs. Do not tell me they are a gift from God. If they are, He should take them back

Japanese role in WWI. Letters, C Savage. Here is a different reminder among all the letters that expressed fear and loathing for the Japanese.

Many a Digger (World War 1 vintage), bound for France from Australia, slept more soundly on board ship, secure in the knowledge that the convoy was safely and efficiently escorted by Japanese war-ships guarding the troopships against the dreaded German U-boats. The Japanese were then our respected allies.

APRIL NEWS ITEMS

Elections back in 1951 were much more exciting and personal than in later years. Politicians stumped round the nation, giving speeches at halls and in parks or at football matches. They were heckled and cheered and sometimes jostled a bit....

One instrument that was often used was **the loudspeaker on the top of cars driving round the town**. They were used by all Parties. How could you be heard in a crowd of a hundred without this device? If opposing rallies were held in adjacent parks, **the obvious way to be heard was to ratchet up the volume until crackling took over**. Some times, the cars carrying loudspeakers ran into each other in the street. Then **they stood 20 yards apart and blared policies at each other....**

Councils across the nation have reacted against this, and said that they will not issue licences to such vehicles unless they "**are used with discretion**".

If you wanted to run **a housie game** in NSW, you needed to apply to Sydney authorities for a licence. This took a long time, and **was a great hassle**, and permission was granted only to the well-known charities. On top of that, prizes could not be in cash, but **only in goods**, such as a doll, a canteen of cutlery, or a set of saucepans....

The NSW Chief Secretary has just allowed a large operator in Sydney to run games every night of the week with half the proceeds used as "expenses for the night", and half to go to a nominated charity. The so-called expense doubtless included a profit for the operator.

Even though prizes are still restricted to goods, it is hoped that this might be **a sign that less restrictive rules might in future apply to housie....**

But not everyone agreed. There were quite a few Letters complaining about this being **the thin edge of the wedge** that would "expose society to the gambling menace."

The US has doubled the number of men in the armed forces in the last nine months. **It now has three million men in uniform.**

The **Lord Mayor of Sydney received a letter of thanks** from 238 students and teachers at **Windemere Grammar school in England.** This was in appreciation of food received by them under the **Council's Food for Britain campaign**.

With the elections coming up, certain cracks in the electoral procedures were becoming obvious. For example, 1,000 passengers who arrived in London on the *Strathnaver* found that **Australia Square did not have any ballot papers....**

It was not possible to get the papers from Australia and then send them back in time for the vote count. Some of them were very cross. An official reminded them that **they could have used an absentee vote before they left Australia. But they were still cross.**

At the end of April, **the stock market was booming** as prosperity caused by **war expenditure** stimulated the entire economy. Commodities were all going well, and wool in particular was still going from record to record.

THE GREAT MOWER WAR

I want you to forget about matters such as looming Federal elections, and Korea. Granted they are important, and we will come back to them in their proper place. **Now**, I want to cover a matter that had more Letters published in the *SMH* than any other in 1951. And as you doubtless guessed, they were all about **electric lawn mowers**.

This wonderful new invention was sweeping the suburbs. Wherever there was a blade of grass, there was an eager man or boy, watching for it to get long enough to cut. As soon as it did, out came the wonderful new gadget, and off with its head.

The old push-and-shove mowers, with their river-boat rotating blades, were gone for good, and the lightweight giant leap in technology was ready for action. Of course, they were quite dangerous in some respects because, being electric meant that a cord had to be dragged behind the mower, and this was always in danger of being cut open by the careless mower. But not at all daunted, hundreds of thousands of households ruined each other's Sunday afternoon nap generating huge numbers of decibels with the help of these contraptions. The only suburban noise to equal it was from the scratching of fountain pens on Sunday night, working out how much was still owed on the mortgage.

Letters, ANTI-NEEDLESS-DIN. Why was a popping motor cycle remaining so long in earshot? I looked out the window and discovered it was a motor mower in a neighbour's garden. The noise continued for several hours.

I have heard several breeds of motor mowers, but never before one like this. It is to be hoped that the new menace to the people's nerve-health will be banned without delay, and the comparative peace of quiet residential areas no longer disturbed by its din.

Letters, O.L.H. I notice that a barrister says that it would cost 200 pounds to take legal action to stop a noisy lawn mower. But if the noise was as bad as that, could not the health officer of a local council abate the nuisance?

Some time ago up the North Shore line, geese were annoying a neighbour and the owners got orders to get rid of them.

Letters, PEACE AND QUIET. Where I live, we have nine mowers of the electric type, and their ceaseless whine on Saturdays and Sundays is something to endure.

If a person tried to earn an honest living with a circular saw making similar noise, the whole of the community would be down on them.

The electricity people frown on a few yards of flex around the house on appliances, yet it seems that any number can be dragged, often on damp ground, to feed these public nuisances.

Letters, H Reid. Manufacturers of electric mowers would, I feel, be well advised to devote some time in designing a real machine that will not only cut grass, but will operate without giving the impression of an air-raid siren.

Letters, Peaceful Sundays. ....the loud popping of the motor became so exasperating that a meeting of nearby residents persuaded the owner to swap it for some thing less irritating. That is how we got rid of this public enemy.

Letter, LOVER OF QUIET. ....One wonders how the nerves of the users of these howling, screaming electric mowers can stand the penetrating, jarring noise.

Surely in this modern, fantastic age, makers can make a machine that is pleasant to the ear. Even the old-type lawnmower, with all its noise, does not sound unpleasant.

Letters, CONTENTED. I prefer the noise or whine for one hour of each week-end to the clatter clatter of the hand-driven machine for the half day that it takes the unlucky male to do the lawn.

Letters, SLEEPLESS ON SUNDAYS. For years I lived in an industrial suburb where weekdays were made unbearable by noise, while the week-end, including the Sabbath, was noticeable for its peace and quiet.

Since coming to live in this select area, I find quite the opposite. The Sabbath is now unbearable, and I wonder whether God has forsaken me. Could He not use His omnipotence to strike these mowers from the face of the earth. Does He not have the power to have the people driving them cut off their own feet.

Then again, perhaps I died and did not notice it at the time, and went to Hell .... yes, yes, I think that's it.

Letters, Manufacturer. Manufacturers will put noiseless electric mowers on the market as soon as they are invented. In the meantime, there is already a noiseless grass-cutter on the market, but it requires chaff and hay to make it work.

Letters, TIRED OUT. As the mother of a young child, I also want silent vacuum cleaners, and washing machines and mixers. I have to do housework at night, or else use the old carpet sweeper and copper. I appeal to someone with a bit of sense.

First Comment. Our cities and suburbs were at the beginning of the noise boom. Somehow, since 1951, we have gradually come to accept levels of noise unheard of back then. We can now live with motor vehicles, chain saws, angle grinders, mixing machines, nail guns, jet planes, surf jets, sirens, and the whole lot. Yet, somewhere in there, someone managed to silence Mister Whippy. Still, where would we be without those noise makers. It is the price we have to pay.

Second comment. Notice that most of the above writers use a pen-name. What it was about this topic to get writers to do that. I can't figure out.

Third comment. Of course, Victa petrol mowers were already on the market, and were happily turning your grass into lawn. But they were more expensive than the electric ones. The electric versions lasted another ten years.

BIG NEWS FROM KOREA

You will recall that MacArthur had proposed doing a Lone Ranger act of meeting the North Korean military leader to end the war. And that his proposal was roundly rejected, and scorned by the powers in Washington. After that, things on the battlefront were as quiet as they can be in a war zone, for about two weeks.

On April 11th, **President Truman sacked MacArthur.** To be precise, he was relieved of his duties as Supreme Commander, Allied Powers in the Pacific, Commander-in-Chief UN Command, US Commander-in-Chief, Far East, and Commanding General, US Army, Far East. He was to step down immediately, and to be replaced by Lieutenant-General Mathew Ridgeway.

The President said he took this step because of MacArthur's inability to give his whole-hearted support to the policies of the American Government. He regretted having to take this step because General MacArthur's place in history as one of the greatest commanders was fully established. When this is translated, it means that MacArthur was keen to extend the war up to the Chinese border and beyond, and Truman thought that would lead to a wider conflict, and saw no reason for this. The straw that broke Washington's back was his unilateral talks proposal of a fortnight ago, and the fact that he had not cleared it with anyone. It is a fundamental precept of western democracy that military operations **must** be subordinated to the elected government. MacArthur was challenging that principle.

Overseas reaction to the dismissal was positive. In Britain, Government supporters cheered the Foreign Secretary when he announced the sacking. Shares on the stock market rose immediately. The Government said it was now hopeful that a peace could be negotiated. In France, peace was also on the mind of the Foreign Affairs Committee. Here, Menzies was non-committal, wanting of course to follow Truman's lead, but compromised because on the previous day he had publicly given MacArthur very generous support.

The General arrived back in the US about a week later. It was agreed that he should address Congress in a few days' time, and after that Truman should respond. In the meantime, the two gentlemen threw a few quiet punches at each other, but both kept their gloves on. MacArthur was a great war hero – more so than Truman – and was very deliberate in courting popular sentiment. Wherever he went, he attracted massive crowds who were generous in their praise and cheers.

When he addressed Congress, he argued he had been put in the impossible situation where, when he had an enemy on the run, he had been instructed not to pursue them. He claimed that this was bad policy, and that he had been supported in this by "practically every military leader concerned with the Korean war." He went on to accuse Truman of blind appeasement and defeatism.

Truman had his say the next day. He quoted military sources that affirmed his policy was the correct one, but he widened the argument by saying that to chase the Reds would certainly have precipitated a Third World War, and that was quite unacceptable. He stood by his view that it was in Europe that the battle against Communism would be won, and that Korea must not become an aggravation that forced the West into a war it did not want. After his speech to Congress, he and other Democrats released some other papers about MacArthur's conduct of the war that were seen to be quite embarrassing to that gentleman's position.

So there the matter rested. It was an unedifying sight to see the President and his top military man embroiled in a public fight of this nature. It was a pity from the Republican point of view that the Presidential elections were not due until the next year, in 1952, because MacArthur, with his millions of supporters, gave them plenty of material to belt the President with.

Comment.   In any case, the war went on, under new management. But tragically, the dreadful incidents that marked it were still happening. As just one example, on March 20th, a Battalion of the Gloucester Regiment stayed put during a vigorous Communist offensive, and refused to withdraw or surrender. After three days without food and water, they were over-run. Only 45 men out of 600 got back to their lines, and the others were posted dead or missing.

Two weeks later, the Battalion received a Presidential Citation, which is America's highest honour for an Army unit, and heaps of praise for their undoubted bravery and their sacrifice. But let me just say, the folly of how they got there in the first place, and the folly of why they would not withdraw, and the folly of anyone who would seek to extend such slaughters, are beyond my understanding.

THE ELECTIONS

There was no doubt that the Liberal Party, in conjunction with the National Party, would be returned to the Lower House. It could be that they might lose a couple of seats in those Labor die-hard areas that had wavered at the previous election, and in other areas there was little scope to gain more because they already held so many. In all, Liberals candidates for the Assembly generally had nothing to worry about.

In the Senate it was a different matter. Each State had 12 seats up for grabs, and the most that any one Party could get was eight of those. Most times the balance would come down as seven seats to five. In some States that had strong working-class affiliations, the scores could well be even. When there was obviously going to be such a small difference between the totals, there was always some doubt as to who would win. The worst thing that could happen for the nation, and the Liberals, was that the

Liberals would win the Lower House, but not get a majority in the Upper. **Surely, not another hung parliament.**

The election campaigns were over and done with in about a month. The Parties offered policies that were in keeping with their previous behaviour. The Liberals promised to get rid of the power of the Reds, and to reform banking. The Labor Party went more for the hip-pocket and promised various breaks for parents and pensioners.

The most glaring difference between the Parties was in how much money they spent on the campaign. The Labor Party said that it was broke, and had no money because it had not expected an election just then, and so had no time to canvas for donors. This is hardly credible given that Menzies had been talking about a double dissolution for a year, and no major legislation had got through Parliament for a year. But that was their claim. In any case, it certainly showed up in newspaper advertising. There were ten times as many adverts for the Libs as for Labor. And the quality was vastly different. The Libs had a range of spicy attractive ads, always hitting some vulnerable point. Their opponents focused on wordy, heavy ads, full of logic. And as anyone can tell you, there is no place at all for logic in an election.

The election was held at the end of April. When the results were all in, Menzies and Government were safely ensconced in both Houses and free to work their magic on the electorate. In particular, they were now geared up to have their way with the dastardly Reds. At last, they would be easy meat

Or would they?

NEWS AND VIEWS

Letters, E Evans, Darwin. Any fool can "break" a horse to saddle and bit, and then jump on his back. But what a sorry sight those animals are to watch when ridden. They have bad head-carriage, are completely unbalanced, and useless for pleasure or work. Their only easy movement is walk in a straight line.

The whole art and object of "breaking" and training a horse is to enable the animal to move at all paces with his balance distributed in such a way that when called upon to execute a manouvre – whether it be a simple turn or something more intricate – he does so with immediate response, ease, grace and control, being perfectly balanced or "collected" at all stages.

This applies to racehorses and cattle horses besides show horses. Too many people seem to be of the opinion that as long as a racehorse will jump out of the gate and gallop with a jockey still on its back, that is all that is required. Too often on the race course do we see horses all but fall down (I permit myself a slight exaggeration), but maybe swerving, bumping, or boring even when going strongly.

I venture to suggest that the reason is that the horse is completely unbalanced. This is probably one of the more frequent causes of horses breaking down – the horse's weight is badly distributed over the ground, thereby imposing greater strain on one or more parts of the anatomy, nearly always the legs.

News for rabid gamblers. A Press report claimed that various promoters of housie-housie are exploiting players and introducing modifications that could well ruin the game. This could happen because players are being encouraged to spend large sums of money on a weekly basis. That will simply benefit the promoters and remove the charitable basis behind the games.

At the moment, each housie function must be approved by the Chief Secretary's Department, and the proceeds must go to places like hospitals, ambulances, churches and other charities. But new operators are moving in and claiming "expenses" that are taking all the gains from the games. They are also charging six pence instead of threepence for a card, and declaring a game over when only one line is completed on the card. Traditionally, it takes the complete card of three lines to declare a game over. Operators are also giving cash prizes, which is illegal, and rely on the fact that games are not generally policed to get away with this. They also build up jack-pots, again illegal, to tens of Pounds.

All of this means that the simple housewife who wants a flutter once a week is being replaced by professional gamblers, with their big gambling money.

At least,that is how the Press report saw it.

In Perth, a flock of pigeons settled on some railway power lines, causing them to sag and touch each other. This **caused a short circuit which killed the pigeons, and blew circuits** through the train network. Many passengers were forced to walk along the track to the next station, and thousands were late for work.

MAY NEWS ITEMS

Potatoes were getting scarce round the nation. Recently, various wages tribunals had granted large wage increases, so it was inevitable that costs of basic goods would rise. For example, 40,000 bags of potatoes have reached Sydney, but will not be available to housewives until a price rise is allowed by the Prices Tribunal. This august body has said that it was in no hurry to lift prices, **and so these potatoes will be put into storage....**

That means that potatoes are getting scarce in the shops. This means that prices will rise anyway, and that **when** the Tribunal officially lifts prices, the rise will be passed on, and so prices will rise yet again. Given that the same is happening to all basic commodities, **no wonder that inflation was a major household worry**.

King George VI had the flu a month ago, and now he has considerable pain in his leg. He **has been advised to relieve himself of some of his dutie**s, but as yet has not done so.

A man in Sydney's Strathfield won **an award of about 100,000 Pounds** from the NSW Supreme Court. He has received, in a single day, **100 begging letters from strangers**. He opened just 20. The beggers wanted to buy, for example, a house, land, a washing machine and a set of false teeth. He threw out the other 80, and has asked the Post Office to not deliver again for a week.

The Very Reverend Dr John Flynn **(Flynn of the Inland)** was famous for his work among Aborigines and establishing the Flying Doctor Service. He died at the weekend in Sydney and was cremated. His ashes will be flown to Alice Springs and scattered over the nearby Mt Gillian.

Japanese newspapers released special editions today to report that **Japan will be allowed to take part in the 1952 Olympic Games** at Helsinki. Japanese officials are surprised and over-joyed that the international community is starting to overlook their past.

A NSW House Member has petitioned the Premier **to allow daylight-saving this year in Winter**. This would lengthen the day in the evening and reduce electricity usage, **and thus cut down on blackouts. Would this also increase the rate at which curtains fade, as it does in the Summer?**

Youths across the nation must **register for National Service by today**. Only 7,000 out of 16,000 have done so as yet. An unusual rule is that **employers who employ an unregistered youth are liable for a fine of 100 Pounds.**

The French Rugby League team is on its way. Keep your guard up. There will be plenty of biffs.

NSW will **introduce long-service-leave** for those covered by **State awards**. This will be similar to that in place for some Commonwealth Public Servants and in some other States. Once an employee reaches **20 years of continuous service** with an employer, **he will be granted three months leave at full pay.**

YOU'RE IN THE ARMY NOW

Start of National Service for young men. One matter that the two major political parties had been able to agree on before the elections was that Australia's military forces needed bolstering. Further, that the way to do that was by forcefully recruiting 18-year-old males, and making them do a term of military service. So, before the ink was dry on the elections, on May 5th, a notice appeared in the nation's daily newspapers.

It required that all young men, aged about 18, should register with the Government in the next ten days. It was known by now that they would be recruited in the New Year for a period of about 13 weeks during which time they would dwell in barracks, and get only a few days leave. They would undergo training in the basics of whatever Service they ended up in, and be paid reasonably for the experience. After the initial training, they would return to civilian life, but they would be required to undergo further training on certain evenings in the Civilian Military Forces, for a period of three years. They would also have to attend a military camp for three weeks for the next three years. Most of the recruits would end up in the Army.

Reaction to this edict was moderate. The idea had become quite familiar because National Service schemes were already in operation in most countries of the Western world.

The young men involved – and I happened to be one of them – were mainly quite happy with it. It seemed to offer a bit of excitement and glamour, and a chance to fool round and act the goat without any serious committment. About ten per cent of lads had not registered by the deadline, but many of these were in the process of doing so, and were given a few days extension. Some mothers were worried that it might all lead to their sons being recruited for overseas service, but such a possibility was specifically excluded at this stage. Elder sisters throughout the nation loved the idea that their indolent useless brothers would get some discipline belted into them. In all, no great controversy erupted, and the lads lined up and registered for their short back-and-sides.

CAN DADS BE PRESENT AT BIRTHS?

News item, May 16th. Mr John Curvers and his wife, Germaine, are at odds with hospitals in Australia. He is from Holland, and she is from Belgium, and she is soon to give birth to their child. The problem is that after contacting many hospitals, they cannot find one that will allow John to be present at the birth. "We pointed out that it was accepted practice in Europe for the father to be present at birth, but they said it was not done here."

The hospital authorities were quite dismayed at the prospect of a father being present. Matron Shaw, of Sydney's Crown Street Women's Hospital, said last night that husbands were **never** admitted to Australian labour wards. "Australian wives would not like that. We have never lost a husband yet. We give them a cup of tea, and send them for a little walk. When they come back, we tell them the news, and they rush away to telephone their friends. If they come back sober, after that we let them see their child."

These attitudes brought forth a great deal of comment.

Letters, NURSE J. Why should we scoff at the **New Australian** who wants to be present at the birth of his child? It seems to me that this is a human right which should not be denied to those who may wants it.

No untrained person should be permitted to usurp the function of the doctor or midwife on such an occasion, except in an emergency, but there can be no doubt that if more husbands had the courage to witness childbirth, there would be a deeper appreciation of the responsibility of parenthood.

Letters, C Kent. What is wrong that a husband should wish to be present at the most wonderful moment of his wife's life. I question Matron Shaw's sweeping statement that "Australian wives would not like it." I feel as Mrs Curvers does, and my husband fully shares my feelings.

If there is a hospital in Sydney which understands the value of a husband's presence during childbirth, and encourages it, then I should be pleased to hear of it.

Letters, Mrs D Dolden. I agree with Nurse J. Surely if the ordeal proved to be too much for our strong male protectors, they could leave the labour ward. I am sure that with the picture of the babe's birth still in his mind, the father would delay his celebrations till he, too, felt like the mother – just a little bit stronger.

Although I would prefer to be alone, there are many women who would prefer the moral support of their husbands' presences.

To doctor and nurses, childbirth is an everyday occurrence, but to husbands and wives it is something that should be very sacred and dear.

Letters, MOTHER OF THREE. Switzerland is another country where the husband is expected to be in the room during his wife's confinement.

I am quite certain that there would be fewer divorces if a husband was allowed to be with his wife and share her experiences, rather than selfishly drink to excess.

Letters, Mother of Five. At my last confinement, it was not till five hours later that my husband knew that he had another beautiful son and that I was feeling exceptionally well.

Letters, EXPECTING MOTHER. I am another New Australian, and am trying hard to understand and adjust myself to Australian ways of life, but there are things on which we cannot change our outlook.

I have explained to doctors that I would like to have my husband with me at the next confinement, and I was looked at as if I was an escapee from a mental hospital. This was now really the worst disappointment I have had in life, for the birth of my second child in a Sydney public hospital was a very unhappy experience, due only to my terrible loneliness and despair.

I am so afraid now of going to hospital, where I will have to say good-bye to my husband at the hospital door in a moment when I would need him most. I often wish I had never come to Australia – at least not for having babies.

Letters, Mrs Belle Carlin. I cannot think of anything more futile than a lot of useless males cluttering up a labour ward at any hospital. Incidentally, they would need to be provided with a gown and mask.

Personally, the thought of any person being present, excepting those necessary, is abhorrent to me. Although not claiming to have populated Australia in the true pioneering spirit, I have three sons on the credit side.

Letters, F A Collins. Clearly it has not occurred to those mothers who are in favour of husbands being present during childbirth that this European custom may not have its origin in either sentiment or chivalry.

Rather is it probably a survival of the old-time exercise of a husband's right to assure himself that the child presented to him is indeed his wife's child.

This, of course, does not alter the fact that some women may derive comfort from the presence of their husbands. On the other hand, other wives may feel that the wish to subject menfolk to this ordeal of witness may spring subconsciously from that age-old feminine resentment of male immunity from the discomfort of bringing a child into the world.

It could be argued, then, that deeper mutual affection is revealed when husband and wife are apart on this vital occasion, and the wife is happy in the knowledge that her spouse is in the good, appropriate company of friends; even though, manlike, he may be drowning his anxiety in his cups.

Letters, SYMPATHISER. As a mother who had to submit to the terrifying experience of having her first babies (twins) in a Sydney public hospital, with a room full of young men and women medical attendants and student nurses looking on, I feel that no hospital should object to the presence of a mere husband.

Letters, S W Krieger, General Secretary, Association of New Citizens. From publicity given to a request by a Dutch migrant to be allowed to be present at his wife's confinement, the impression may have been gained that the presence of husbands in labour wards is an established practice all over Europe.

Nothing is further from the truth. On the very rare instances, where husbands make such a request, it will depend on a doctor's approval.

The majority of European obstetricians are certainly not encouraging that practice, though in some cases permission might be granted for psychological reasons.

Generally speaking, the Australian practice is also that observed in Europe.

Comment. My, how things have changed. It would appear from these Letters, and other material, that the impetus for this change came primarily from our New Australian friends. In these Letters, Australian mothers-to-be are not very vocal, and I suspect they were fairly ambivalent about the changes at that time. Note the constant referral to the dad going off to the pub, to "wet the baby's head." Maybe this has changed a bit now too.

MORE ON KOREA

I had hoped that I could say that nothing happened in the Korean saga. And to some extent, nothing spectacular did. In America, Truman and MacArthur continued their campaigns against each other but, with Truman having all the resources of the Government behind him, MacArthur was gradually losing his appeal. In the UN, at America's behest, an embargo was placed on the sale of certain war materials to China and North Korea. But given that Russia was not included in this embargo, it was not hard to work out just how effective it would be.

In the background, the war went on. In the air, daily the USA would send off its bombers in the hundreds to destroy "strategic" targets. On the ground, the two armies sometimes went forwards a few miles and then, next day, they went back. In the process, thousands of men were killed and maimed, and life went on, for some, as normal.

I hope that next month there is **nothing** to report on Korea.

MENZIES' BATTLE WITH THE REDS

The New Zealand wharfies were out on strike, and had been for a couple of months. During this period Australian workers had sent money as strike pay to NZ, and this pittance was gratefully accepted. But **now**, the NZ Government called in the troops to work the NZ wharves, so the Australian wharfies and seamen put a black ban on handling NZ ships.

"Thank you very much", cried Bob Menzies, because now he had cause to belt the living daylights out of the Commos who led the Waterside Workers Federation (WWF) and the Seamens' Union. His first effort was to have Commonwealth Security Police raid the premises of these two Unions, and seize papers and make a mess. The wharfies struck for a day in protest, and still refused to work NZ vessels. Menzies called in troops to load the NZ ship *"Port Halifax"*, and the Secretary of the WWF was charged with four offences under the Crimes Act.

It all happened so quickly, and the speed, and the use of the Crimes Act, signalled that Menzies was determined to make a major issue out of it. We will come back to this battle next month. But, we should remember that Menzies was at the same time planning his next move in furthering his anti-red Bill through Parliament. It too will soon come back to thrill and tickle your fancy.

AUSTRALIA'S DEFENCES

After each of the two Worlds wars, our armed services were de-mobbed, and we were left with just a rump of seasoned military officers and men to run our military establishment.

By 1951, the international situation had changed, and our political leaders were saying that we needed to build up our military again. This was mainly because of the situation that was fast developing in Korea where the Reds were forever increasing their military efforts to bring light and reason to South Korea.

So, lucky lads aged 18 were about to be mustered and given military training. They were not to be sent overseas, but they would provide some resistance and help if military necessity demanded it. Every young lad of the right age was invited to attend, and indeed faced fines and gaol if he did not.

Of course, exemptions were allowed. The physically impaired were exempt. Others who professed to have religious scruples could be conscripted for non-fighting roles. But in general, when the system was in full swing, most young men went to the party. Of course, this compulsion was made politically easier because none of the young warriors had a vote as yet.

To most of the young men, this was no real chore. It was rather good fun to go off for three months initially, to play soldiers with real guns and grenades. And, as it turned out, to learn a little discipline and something of social responsibility. To some participants, myself included, it was an experience not to be missed.

NEW NUMBER PLATES

Letters, DISGUSTED OWNER. I would like to register a very strong protest in regard to the colour schemes adopted by the NSW Transport Department for the new vehicle number plates with their bright yellow and black colours.

Every vehicle owner to whom I mention the matter is in agreement with me that they are an eyesore and ruin the appearance of most vehicles to which they are attached. The white on black plates toned in with the dignity of all vehicles.

Letters, Neil McQueen. I agree with the criticism of these ghastly yellow number plates.

Motorists pay a great deal for the appearance of their cars, and should not have to put up with their disfigurement at the whim of the Transport Department. Is it too late to have them recalled?

Letters, J Mack. The responsible Minister should recall these monstrosities and urge the education of the officials concerned in an aesthetic sense. Far too many bureaucrats seem intent on despoiling our fair city, which was formerly one of the most beautiful in the world.

RIPENING OF FRUIT

Everyone nowadays complains that fruit is not as tasty as it was years ago. And we all know that they now pick fruit in glut time, and pump it full of gas, and keep it in cold storage until customers get desperate enough to eat it. Well, I have included a few letters to inform you that these tricks are not all that new.

Letters, H Batt, Coastal Citrus Growers Marketing Association. May I point out that oranges are coloured by being subjected to 48 hours in the ethylene chamber, which dissolves the chlorophyll in their skin. The real crime is they are picked in an immature state, often bottle green.

The branding of cases is useless to stop the practice. Some are unscrupulous, while others are forced by economic circumstances to adopt this method of obtaining a price commensurate with production costs. We, as a committee have the objective of stamping out this practice of colouring early navels. We will use statutory power to do this. In the US, under the Pure Foods and Drugs Act Decision No 133, the colouring of citrus is prohibited.

Letters, Professor Marcus Oliphant, Australian National University. Mr Batt is in error when he states that the artificial colouring of oranges is prohibited in the US. I have purchased several of the eastern States oranges on which was stamped "Artificially coloured", and well remember the sniggers of the California Fruit Control Officers who found these in my possession when crossing the Arizona border.

Sales of coloured oranges, like that of coloured margarine, is forbidden in some States, but in the latter case a packet of suitable dye is enclosed.

NEWS AND VIEWS

The new beer gardens. Letters, Brian Udhy. Not so long ago one of the new "beer gardens" was created in a Sydney suburb. We expected to see cleaner drinking with more restraint, but were disappointed.

It is really tragic to see the number of young people and mothers with children who take their drink under these "better conditions".

Such beer gardens have brought drink closer to the home and our children, and any proposal to make drink more easily accessible to the immature person can only add more difficulties to an already serious situation.

Comment: Despite complaints from a few people, the new beer gardens were getting a great deal of acceptance. In fact, most complaints were directed at the noise generated rather than at the dubious claims of excessive consumption.

News item, Sydney, June 16ᵗʰ. The Minister for Labour, Mr P Finnan, introduced a Bill into the NSW Legislative Assembly that will provide **long-service leave to State employees** for the first time. The provision initially sought is for 12 weeks leave after 20 years of service, though this may well change as the Bill is argued though the Chamber.

The bill also seeks to give tribunals power to **grant preference to unionists over non-unionists**, and abolishes the three shillings a week differences between city and country wages.

The Opposition Leader, Mr Treatt, bemoaned the fact that the Bill did not provide for secret ballots on strike issues.

Comment. This Bill was obviously a step forward for workers. Looked at today, the requirement for 20 years of service seems harsh. Still, in those days, the work-force was much more stable. People often had "jobs for life", and 20 years working with the same company was common.

Letters, LEFT-HANDER. Prince William is reportedly having his hair parted on the right side instead of the left – the usual side for boys.

It may not be generally known that the natural growth of hair on the human head is such that a so-called "crown" is formed on top of the head, towards the back. This crown is located slightly on the left-hand side, hence a parting from the crown to the front of the head will fall in an easy and natural manner.

In a few cases, however, the crown appears on the right-hand side {probably associated with left-handedness) and in such case the natural and easy parting should be on the right-hand side, otherwise there is apt to be an untidy tuft of hair sticking up from the artificial crown created by left-hand parting.

Radio Programmes. Of course, this was well before the golden age of television. So that the evenings were spent in front of a radio cabinet or a new-fangled portable radio, listening to 15-minute serials.

For example, in the period from 6 to 7 pm, listeners to 2GB got *Nick Carter, Biggles,* and *Superman.* On 2UW, there was the classic pairing of *Martin's Corner* and *Dad and Dave.* 2CH had the impossible-to-miss *Yes What.*

In the next hour, you had the choice of *The News, Hagan's Circus, When a Girl Marries,* and *Courtship and Marriage.*

Most stations closed down about 11pm. And most of them finished the day with a religious message or meditation of a couple of minutes.

JUNE NEWS ITEMS

2,000 youths failed to register for National Service in NSW. They will be given **one week's grace.** If they fail, then they **will be fined 50 Pounds**, and their names will still be registered for them.

Butter production is down in Australia because of floods and droughts. We do have a large quantity in stock, but that is contracted to be sent to Britain So we come to the remarkable **situation where we are talking about importing butter.**

The English soccer team is touring Australia and **due to play Tasmania today.** This morning, the local Club found that **thousands of pieces of glass** had been spread on the oval by vandals. The Club called for **volunteers** to clean the sward, and **two hundred people** turned out and **spent their morning picking up every shaft.** The match started on time.

John Curtin was an honest and **much-loved Prime Minister** of this nation till his death over a year ago. **His widow will receive a Parliamentary Pension of five Pounds per week** from his super fund. Any other pension she might receive will be reduced to allow for this sum.

Comment. I shake my heard when I think of this. Surely we could have done a lot better.

The well-regarded medical journal, called the *General Practitioner*, warned men of the **dangers of waistcoats.** It said **that vests constrict the chest** and do not allow the free passage of air. "Fortunately, the waist-coat is disappearing, but in colder climates like Melbourne, the unhealthy habit persists...."

But, don't panic. The waistcoat might still be acceptable. A spokesman for the BMA said that he would always stand by the **waistcoat as an essential part of men's clothing**. "No waistcoat can do harm while the wearer is comfortable in it."

Comment. Whatever happened to fob pockets? And, what about **fob watches and chains?** I bet that half my readers can't even remember them....

It is interesting that in 2016, waistcoats are making **a comeback**. This time they are as **a fashion garment**, and not for warmth as previously. **So too are braces**.

In Sydney, newspapers carried a small front-page panel that told of **the electricity situation**. It described what happened yesterday, and what might be expected today. On June 23rd , it said "Half of Zone A was blacked out from 8.16am to 8.46. One tenth of Zone B from 5.23 till 5.52." **The Commissioner said that things were good and "today was the best day of this week...."**

June 26th however, was **the worst day on record** since zoning started on April 30th. Blackouts started in some zones at 6.30am, and finished in other zones, or the same zones, at 9.30pm . The Commissioner again: "it was a very dirty day indeed. The worst we have had...."

The Commissioner went on to remind householders that the use of radiators was illegal. "Every time a radiator is switched on, 20 house lights must go off...."

BURGESS, MacLEAN

On June 7th, London and Paris newspapers carried a small story about two diplomats who were missing from their posts. The British Foreign Office indicated that an international hunt was underway for the two men, and that it was thought that they had made their way to the Continent.

The first of these, Donald MacLean, was Head of the American Department of the British Foreign Office. The second, Guy Burgess, was on leave from the British Embassy in Washington. Both of these men were in high ranking positions, and moved in circles that were well informed about the various policies of Government. It was thought that they may have information that was of value to the Russians, though there was no evidence that any vital papers were missing. Neither person had been seen since they left their homes on May 25th, but there was nothing to suggest that they had been forced to leave.

The next day the Press, now getting quite excited, reported that friends and colleagues were confident that the two missing men were on a "spree" in Paris. They knew the men to be men-about-town who were well known in London café and club society. Both were members of the Gargoyle Club, a place notorious for players and stayers. They also knew Paris intimately, including some of its most unconventional nightlife. The *Daily Herald* added that Burgess held Communist views while at University, and remained a close student of Communism after he joined the Foreign Office.

By June 9th, the heat was really on. It was now thought that they were in Warsaw, in Poland. The papers reported that between 10,000 and 15,000 "police and counter-espionage agents are combing West Europe for the men." If they were in Warsaw, it was speculated, MacLean should be easy to spot because he was six feet, four inches tall. Were they on the run, with a well thought-out plan of concealment, and headed for the Soviet Union?

By June 10th, the BBC, at the request of the Foreign Office, broadcast the biggest SOS ever put on air, to 19 European countries over six high-powered stations. It was a description of the missing men, and an appeal to report them to the local police if they were seen.

But to no avail. On June 11th, Bucharest Radio, the official mouthpiece of the Russian Cominform propaganda body, said that the pair had reached Prague by air. From that, it seemed highly likely that the two men **had** defected, and were by now eating caviar and Russian crabs in Moscow or wherever.

For almost a week, the world's newspapers had been completely dominated by this spy story. All the nefarious dreamings of hundreds of writers of books and radio plays had been realised. Two privileged and prominent swanks, Cambridge educated, had defected behind the Iron Curtain, after years of transmitting State secrets to the vile Russians, and thrown their hats in with the Commos.

How did they deceive their selection panels for their jobs? How did they manage to keep their jobs, all the way through the War, and in that period, transmit top-level information to Russia in huge volumes? Where were the counter-espionage sections of the famous British MI5, and the more secretive MI6, all this time? The best that can be said for them was that they had woken up to Guy Burgess, and he was to face an internal please-explain panel three days after he disappeared. But, he wisely chose not to turn up for questioning.

So the affair ended. The Brits' Secret Service had not just eggs on their face, but an entire chookyard. These defections started a large run of such events, into Russia and out of Russia, with both sides claiming propaganda victories every time someone changed sides. In Australia, we had our own Petrov sell out, though he was a baddie changing over to us goodies.

One consequence for Australia of these shenanigans was that ASIO, just struggling into existence, came up against a public who were simply not at all convinced that these spy organisations were worth their money. Another consequence was that Bob Menzies was placed further on the back-foot in his efforts to get atomic secrets out of America. There was, in fact, no chance that he would ever do so, but the US used the British security fiasco to make the point that any secrets given to Australia – as part of the British Empire – would not be in safe hands. **No way, Jose.**

Absolute trivia. In 1983, the grandson of MacLean married the great-great-niece of Burgess in Dayton, USA.

SPLENDID TIMES IN CANBERRA

Canberra, Tuesday, June 12th. The 20th Commonwealth Parliament was opened today with pomp and pageantry to **celebrate the 50th anniversary of the Federation.** This was the grandest and most ceremonious event in the nation's history since the King and Queen (then the Duke and Duchess of York) opened the first Federal Parliament to sit in Canberra in 1927.

During the ceremony, the Governor-General took the salute from a march-past of 3,600 Servicemen and Nurses. A fly-past of RAAF fighters was cancelled because of expected rain and storms.

The place was alive with dignitaries. Of course, the Prime Minister and the Leader of the Opposition were there, both of them busy welcoming the guests. Apart from the Members of both Houses of Parliament, and the Governor-General, William McKell, there were all the judges of the High Court and four US Congressmen, and the Prime Minister of New Zealand and his wife.

Four State Governors, the Chief Justice, Premiers of Six States, and the heads of Churches in Australia also attended. The entire Diplomatic Corps occupied spots on the floor of the Chamber.

The crowd kept growing. Also present were the Chancellor of the Duchy of Lancaster, Lord Alexander, and the Lord Lieutenant of the County of Durham, Lord Lawson, representing the British Government. The most picturesque figure was the Indian High Commissioner who wore a large green and red silk turban, a high-collared frockcoat, and tight-fitting white trousers. The official representatives for

Indonesia and for Pakistan were there, and wore traditional Muslim gear. Also there was the Russian Ambassador and his wife.

The ceremony was opened by famous singer Marjorie Lawrence, who sang the Lord's Prayer from the steps of Parliament House.

In the evening, the front of Parliament House was flood-lit, showing up the large array of international flags that festooned the building surrounds. There was a display of fireworks on Capital Hill. And wives of Members were welcome to attend a "Night of Opera", by New Australians in the Albert Hall.

Last night, 372 guests attended a State banquet, and it was repeatedly stated that all the guests mixed very freely and a good time was had by all.

Tonight, there will be a Jubilee Ball, and the guests invited are much the same as at last night's banquet. It is expected that the conviviality shown at last night's function will extend to this evening's prance.

Comment. This was a gathering that was unprecedented in Australia's history. Everyone who was anyone was there. The banquet the previous night was rated a great success by all, and the Opening of Parliament was a gala occasion to remember. **Now all that remained was the Jubilee Ball to top off the whole Jubilee calendar.**

Mr. CHIFLEY DIES FROM SEIZURE

Press statement. "Mr Chifley frequently did not attend gala functions, preferring simpler pleasures. He chose not to attend the Jubilee Ball because he was somewhat tired from the Dinner the previous night. He had retired early to bed, and was reading some newspapers brought to him by Miss Phillis Donnelly, who was his companion and typist. When the seizure first took place, he made light of it, and did not want a doctor called. Miss Donnelly insisted. A doctor immediately made arrangements for Mr Chifley to go to hospital. On the way, he fell into a coma, and was given oxygen, but he died on the journey."

Mr Menzies was informed of these events, and he passed them on to the Ball in solemn tones. He said that the Ball was now abandoned. A hush descended on the guests, and many people, both men and women, broke into tears.

Mr Menzies' announcement said: "It is my sad duty to tell you that tonight, during this celebration, Mr Chifley, former Prime Minister, and Leader of the Opposition, has died. I do not want to even try to talk about him because, although we were political opponents, he was a great friend of yours and mine, and a fine Australian.

"It does not matter about party politics in a case like this. Oddly enough, in Parliament we get to know each other very well, and we sometimes feel that we have a warmest friendship among people whose politics are not our own.

"He has served his country and undoubtedly has hastened his own passing by his devotion to his own land, and indeed, to the people of the world."

Mr Chifley, aged 65, was given a State funeral and buried at his home city of Bathurst.

MORE KOREA

The Korean War showed little change. Some serious attempts were being made in the UN to get a settlement, and perhaps were making headway. But these were hindered by the fact that, though all parties to the War were fed up with it, and were very keen to get out of it, no one wanted to be seen to be backing down. The Russian chief delegate to the UN made a serious proposal for a peace, and that was being given cautious consideration by the West.

In the meantime, the UN and Communist troops were in their battle lines. For the time being at least, it appeared that the fun of pushing forwards and backwards over the same terrain had lost its appeal, and the troops were digging in. This, of course, made a lot more sense, and hopefully more of them would stay alive while the diplomats and politicians in Washington and Moscow and the UN continued their point-scoring exercises.

THE RED MENACE

Menzies had a wonderful month frustrating the wharfies. Every time they played a card, he trumped it. They refused to man ships in Melbourne, and in Queensland, so he put in troops, and civilian volunteers. The seamen refused to man a New Zealand ship, so he brought in naval ratings. He charged four more Union officials under the Crimes Act. He was everywhere, and dominated the scene.

It even got to the stage that when Healey was brought to Court for a preliminary hearing, the wharfies Union told their members **not** to strike for that day. About one hundred workers **did strike, and they were admonished and fined by the Union. Can you believe that? Fined for striking.**

Then, as usual, the strike was settled, and that only left Healey to face the Court next month under the Crimes Act.

END THE HOUSING SHORTAGE?

Housing shortage. Press report, June 20th. Since the end of the War, and the start of the Baby Boom, there had been a large unsatisfied demand for new houses for new families. By 1951, demand was being fuelled because by now many people had had enough time to accumulate the deposit that the banks required, and because everyone was getting good wages, and so could readily afford the repayments. But supplies were not increasing all that much and so such schemes as the one below were instigated to ease the shortage.

Pre-fabricated housing from England. A British firm expects to deliver 5,000 new pre-fab houses to NSW early next year. The NSW Housing Commission has negotiated a deal with Taylor Woodlow P/L for a price of ten million Pounds. The vendors will do what they can to avoid "awful uniformity" by having them face in different directions, and by having them in five different colour schemes. They will also have wide eaves to accommodate the large amount of sunlight that Australia expects. They would all be single story, and light steel-framed, with timber floors, doors, ceilings, walls, and partitions.

Comment. It was a good idea, but one that received little notice at the time.

NEWS AND VIEWS

Train Travel. Letters, A Kater, Trangie. I would like to draw your attention to the way our country children who attend boarding school in Sydney are treated by NSW Government Railways.

This term, we tried to book seats on sleepers 10 days ahead, and were told all seats and sleepers were booked out. Parents at other stations were able to book seats on the day that the train left. However, those who joined the train further down the line had the same seats booked, and in the arguments which followed, the guard displaced the unfortunate long-distance ones, whose parents were not there to back them up.

With 11 children in a compartment with six seats on a bitterly cold night, the older sisters put the little ones to bed on the corridor floors. However, an unfeeling gentleman insisted that the lights remain on all night.

Many of these country children travel 400 miles to school, and have all of the day and most of the night to travel.

The Country Women's Association has urged that special school carriages be supplied, with a hostess in charge. This matter has been brought up in the Legislative Council, but no lasting improvements have been effected.

Letters, OLD-TIMER. Surely the Railway Department owes it to long-suffering suburban train travellers to lessen the jungle scramble into the trains. A few special officers should be appointed, with a roving commission, to see that intending passengers stand several feet from the train until outgoing ones have emerged, and to encourage the public to keep to the left in big subways.

My wife was knocked down and injured by some burly ruffians pushing their way into the carriage before she alighted. Surely we can recover some semblance of civilisation.

Letters, BUTTER-BEFORE-DRIPPING. I have no doubt that many of the digestive ills of to-day can be traced to the dripping-instead-of-butter diets of the last century. If it was economic necessity that dictated the use of dripping on toast, there was an excuse for it. If not, it appears to me as an unnecessary exercise of thrift.

Comment. The use of dripping, instead of butter, was still common enough in 1951, especially with families that had a large number of children. Though I was lucky enough to live in a family that always had butter, I can remember neighbours who were not. Interestingly, though, when I tried some of their fare, it was not too bad. It depended on what meats and bacon that the dripping had been cooked down from. It could be quite delicious.

One cleric's opinion on morals. Letters, Illado. Cardinal Gilroy's damnation of intoxicating liquor at dances, and also of "beach dances", will find a ready echo from many members of all denominations.

The heads of the Churches cannot too often speak of the evils that are sapping and undermining our Christian standards. In many ways, **housie-housie** is just as detrimental as starting-price betting, and causes women to neglect their homes and children.

JULY NEWS ITEMS

Give me a break. Housewives right round the nation are being frustrated by the shortage of potatoes for **all sorts of reasons**. Now the Potato Board of Tasmania has found a **wonderful new excuse** to add to its list of incompetencies. It says that, though there is a good crop of new potatoes being dug up, **it does not have enough sacks for them**. The result: a continued shortage of spuds.

I will add just one more item to **the housewives laments**, and then stop. **Soap is in short supply**, and is being unofficially rationed. Even bars of Sunlight soap. And even the new **washing powders** replacing Sunlight.

Several reports from the Northern Territory indicate that the Aborigines are becoming aware of the value of crocodile skins and are now organising blockades of the rivers against white poachers....

"Armed canoes were strung across a river, and the white men were **threatened with dozens of spears** when they attempted to force their way through."

Comment. This *SMH* report closed with the footnote. "**Arnhem Land natives are the most dangerous in the nation.** Several tribal leaders have been accused of murder, and before the war, several other natives were punished for the massacre of a Japanese lugger crew, and the murder of a NT police officer."

Second comment. I am not sure that this collection of scattered facts adds up to the conclusion that Arnhem Land natives were particularly dangerous.

A lone miner on Cape York Peninsula fell down a well. A dingo had access to the shaft through a small tunnel. The miner was stunned and injured and the dingo mauled him badly. The man recovered, and clambered up a ladder. He returned to his camp, got his rifle, and shot the dingo from the top of the well.

Comment. Life in some parts of Australia was still pretty primitive.

It appears that **Lana Turner** in the US has been voted "the **most glamorous woman in the history of international art**." This was by the Academy of Contemporary Arts, an organisation of painters, sculptors, and illustrators. Most impressive. Yet, **I wonder how they came to that conclusion.**

The Australian Stevedoring Industry Board's purpose in life was to try to bring **some sanity into the non-stop warfare between wharfies and ship-owners**. It did its job about as well as most Boards in Australia, and **was thus not widely praised**....

It did however, break out of its lethargy and reported in July that many **wharfies were wasting** about a third of their time on the job, and that their supervision was woeful. For example, many were found playing cards or fishing, many were absent from the job without the supervisor caring, and quite a few did their day's drinking while rostered on. It also resented the attitude among employers that regarded the Board as an interloper without purpose or importance. **Comment.** This made bad headlines, but nothing changed.

PERSIAN OIL

In the meantime, across the world, another **epoch-making event** was gradually unfolding. The Arab world and the so-called Middle East, were waking up to the fact that it was providing much of the world's oil, but was getting only a pittance in return. Persia, now called Iran, was the first post-War nation to act on this, and in 1951 had set out to rectify the situation.

The British had been pumping oil from Persia for more than 50 years, and had gained access to this oil by paying a royalty. Now, the Persians wanted to turn the whole situation round, and take most of the revenue for themselves, and pay the British a royalty. They were quite happy to keep the British workers there to run the facilities, and were equally happy to pay a rental on those facilities, all as part of a royalty. But their Prime Minister, Mussadiq, and his government, were adamant that they wanted the biggest part of the pie.

The Anglo-Iranian Oil Company, which had operated the fields for years, were not at all receptive to this idea. They passed it on to the British Government, and it too was quite cool on it. The other colonial powers and America, all of whom had similar fields round the world, could see the writing on the wall and they also wanted to squash the whole concept.

So it came down to a game of bluff and swagger. Everyone tried to negotiate for six months, and they ended up with a few concessions here and there. But there were all sorts of aggravations and provocations on both sides. For example,

Averill Harriman, the US Presidential Adviser, flew in to Abadan as an ace arbitrator, and was met with two days of rioting in the streets. The Brits moved two cruisers off the coast, and they patrolled up and down within sight of the refineries for months, simply reminding the Persians that if the situation came to blows, then the Brits had the upper hand. The matter was placed before the World Court, but the Arabs refused to accept its decision, and then put it to the UN, which sat on it because so many nations had their own interests in the decision. So, by the end of July, the Persians had expelled half the British, and looked like taking over the whole operation.

But the principle, that **the Arabs should have ownership of the oil under their land**, had not been conceded. The counter argument, that **the fields had been developed by foreign money, and that this gave the ownership to the foreigners**, was still the stance taken by the foreign powers. The acceptance of the Arabs' position, over the next few decades, came slowly and reluctantly, but it did come. The net result, obviously, was that the world is now more or less at the mercy of Middle East oil. And that those countries in the region that are oil-rich are now undergoing a renaissance where untold wealth is being poured into their coffers.

THE KOREAN DEBATE

All attention was now on negotiations. There were two new developments here. **Firstly,** the talks moved from the UN headquarters in New York to the 38th parallel in Korea, right in the middle of the current battle zone. That meant that the negotiators had some chance of knowing what they were talking about. **Secondly,** discussion was now moving towards establishing a neutral de-militarised zone between the two nations. Such a zone might be close to the 38th parallel, and be several miles wide so that the two nations of Korea could glare at each other from a distance.

So during July, these armistice talks went on. Every day, both sides would issue Press statements that said "We are the good guys. The other guys are all baddies. If they keep being bad, we will reluctantly walk away. But, nobly, we are sticking it out for the moment."

Alas, the UN issued the following statement on July 31st. "Relations have improved, and we are considering the establishment of a zone to separate the two sides. **In the meantime, combat is still continuing.**"

So perhaps peace was round the corner. But not right now, for the troops in the trenches. Every few days, from one side or the other, a few Companies would rush forward, 50 would be killed, and then they would return to their lines, happy in the knowledge that they had done their bit for the goodies. I look forward to, perhaps next month, when I might include a by-line that says "Combat has been **suspended** while negotiations are continuing."

HEALEY GAOLED

Sentence was passed on the Waterside Worker's Secretary, James Healey. He had transgressed the Crimes Act by recommending that workers put a black ban on loading goods for New Zealand. He was sentenced for two periods of six-weeks gaol, to be served concurrently, and fined 100 Pounds.

By now, the workers in NZ were back at work, and the strike appeared to have been futile. One thing stood out from all the hubbub that surrounded the incidents. Now that Menzies had full control of Parliament, he was determined and ruthless in his pursuit of Communism, in whatever form it appeared. He could easily have had these charges against Healy withdrawn when the strike collapsed. But he did not. He continued with them all the way, and was quoted as being "satisfied" that Healey was gaoled. **Watch out, folks. This Menzies bloke, even though he is new in the job, could be a force to contend with.**

HIRE PURCHASE

A new type of loan financing was gaining popularity in Australia. Under Hire Purchase, you could organise a moderate-sized loan for yourself, with low security, and a short pay-out period, through a company that was not so difficult to deal with as the sanctimonious banks. For this privilege, you had to pay a **true** rate of interest of about 16 per cent. People in their thousands were flocking into the HP Companies to get loans for electric refrigerators, motor cars, and all sorts of appliances. Their idea was that they could have the use of it now, and pay it off over a few years. Since most people then had job security, and good wages, they were happy to sacrifice the interest they paid for the utility of having the object a few years earlier.

The Companies that provided this facility raised their money by selling debentures to the public, again paying an attractive rate of interest, and then lending it out at a higher rate. Some prominent names which enjoyed this boom were Custom Credit, Cambridge Credit, and Beneficial Finance

Corporation. About 20 years and 30 years later, when some of them got into financial trouble, the banks were waiting to take them over, and now the banks market virtually the same product as personal loans, or as extensions to mortgages.

Now, in 1951, this new financial product was in the hot seat, and there were some in the community who had doubts about it. But, equally, there was a multitude of supporters.

Letters, O Bisset. It is apparently assumed by certain bankers that Hire Purchase is wholly objectionable and should be suppressed. One wonders whether this is correct.

Mr and Mrs A are a young couple expecting a baby about the middle of next summer and, quite reasonably, want a refrigerator. There are two alternatives. They can either get one now through HP, or they save for a couple of years and go through the next two summers without a refrigerator. Mr A decides that he can find the eight shillings a week instalments by cutting out a five shilling bet, and having three less beers. Is that wrong?

Similarly, Mrs B is elderly, and the washing is getting too much for her. She would finance a washer by not going to the pictures. If she waits three years, she might be dead. Is she wicked? Mr C's house has cost more than planned. Should he live in it for three years without furniture, or get it now and pay for it out of income? Mr D's car is dead. He cannot do his job without a car. He can get one on HP. What is he to do?

The fact is that HP is diversionary rather than inflationary. It diverts money from betting, beer, and pictures to articles for use. Is that objectionable?

Without wishing to be cynical, one has the feeling that the people who oppose HP are already the owners of all the refrigerators etc that they want. Or they can get them by means of a bank overdraft. Any curtailment of HP would be anti-social and in any case would probably not result in a spectacular increase in savings.

Letters, C Heaton. We bankers do not find HP totally objectionable, but we do consider it undesirable in the present circumstances.

Inflation means that the aggregate effective demand of the community is in excess of the aggregate supply, thus any policy that increases effective demand only adds to the inflation. Mr Bisset would certainly object if Sir Arthur Fadden announced a budget deficit for the coming year. But in the same way, HP means that thousands of people can have a personal budget deficit. They are spending more than they earn. And this is inflationary.

Letters, I B. I wish to thank Mr Bisset for speaking on HP on behalf of those for whom HP is a blessing.

I arrived in this country from England about eleven months ago with wife and three young children. We had to sell our furniture in England, as it is much too expensive to bring over. All we brought was our personal belongings and our savings amounting to just 800 Pounds.

We managed to buy a fibro cottage through a building society with our savings as a deposit. Although we spent all of our money on the house, we were yet able to buy the most essential furniture, like a baby cot, beds for the boys and ourselves, mattresses, table and chairs. Thanks to the HP system, we got these when we needed them.

We also bought a HP wireless-set. I suppose those preaching that the system should be abolished would call us unduly extravagant.

SUNDAY SPORT

Letters, (Rev) R Hicken, St Paul's Rectory, Sydney.
All friends of Rugby Union, who are also pledged to the Christian faith, will regret the decision to play football on a Sunday.

Australia has a Christian inheritance. Our roots are still in the historic faith, though we do not always remember it. If we are to remain a Christian country, which is another thing, we shall have to refrain from trifling with institutions such as the Christian Sunday. Sporting bodies, with players drawn from all groups in the community, ought to be guided by public interest in this matter.

It is unfair to place upon keen young men **the necessity of choice** between loyalty to Christian principle and playing Rugby Union. Those, like myself, who are closely associated with groups of men and boys in Church life, know how great a part sport plays, and rightly so, in their activities.

They ought not be robbed of representation in the big matches simply because those who arrange them decide to jettison tradition. Nor is it right to place such a temptation before them that their love of sport conflicts with the love of God. That this is involved in the secularisation of Sunday is clear to all who have Christian fellowship with young men.

Comment. This is similar in a way to the controversy that occurred the previous year when international tennis was played at White City on a Sunday. But then it was for true champions, including overseas stars, with a crowd of thousands. Here, it was for local lads, with only their families perhaps to watch. It looked like the thin edge of the wedge, and that it could become part of the regular scene. And in Rugby Union at that. But, fortunately, the might of the Supreme Court was at hand.

Letters, (Justice) Herron, Judge's Chambers, Supreme Court, Sydney. I was not present at the meeting when it was decided to play a football match on a Sunday, but in fairness it should be stated that **no** decision was reached that Rugby Union football should be played on a Sunday **as a general rule**. The match under discussion was an isolated instance of a game which had to be played on account of bad weather, and it was thought that there was no alternative but to play on a Sunday.

Since learning of the decision, I have taken steps to see that the match be not played on a Sunday. May I also assure your readers that **while I am President, Sunday football will not be sanctioned by the Rugby Union.**

Further comment. Of course, all sports, including Rugby Union, play games on Sundays nowadays. And this is true for juniors right up to Test match level. It seems that our young folk no longer have the same conflict of interest that they once had, because many of them simply do not go to church at all. And, it should be noted, we have a much more heterogeneous society, where there are many more citizens who do not espouse the Christian religion and traditions.

A NEW ANTHEM?

Letters, John Sturdy. Recently a Senator proposed we look at getting a different national anthem from *God Save the King*. This seems to be long overdue, and I will tell you why.

That song is too much like a hymn. If you listen to hymns and prayers, they are silly. Take the *Hail Mary*. "Blessed art thou amongst women". Take the *Father's*

Prayer. "Hallowed be thy name." Are Jesus and Mary so insecure that they need to be told this time and time again? Surely not. What are they supposed to get out of all those prayers to them. **I bet they are bored stiff.** Now to *God Save the King*. "Long to reign over us." Is that what everyone in the Empire wants? What about those colonies that are now struggling for independence. And what about all the black men? Do they want a white man for ever to reign over them? Surely not.

Advance Australia Fair is the best we have at the moment. Maybe we should have a national contest to seek an anthem. I would suggest *Waltzing Matilda*, except everyone I say that to thinks I'm mad. But we need to change away from what we have now.

Now that I've got everyone off-side, let me add that we should stop playing the anthem at all public events like picture shows. Are we so insecure that we need this type of support?

Letters, John Bulb. Mr Sturdy's recent letter offers gratuitous insults to the King, and blasphemy to God and the Virgin Mary. I will dismiss these statements with the contempt they deserve.

"God save the King" uses exalted words that may or not be true. They are used, not to be taken literally, but as an expression of the exalted status he has among the singers and among his subjects. I do not know with what authority Mr Sturdy speaks for "black men", but I suggest that the fact that the Empire is still the leading example of international co-operation in the world suggests that these "black men" as a whole are not clamouring to get out of the Empire. I can tell you with certainty that the King, and all the institutions that come with him, is vastly superior to anything some fledgling colony will come up with. **God Save the King.**

NEWS AND VIEWS

Letters, Michael Sawtell. The RSPCA or police, I suggest, ought to instruct some of the drivers of horse-drawn vehicles in the city how to drive humanely. I repeatedly see some new-chum driver with his hands wide apart, urging his horse forward with one rein and tugging at the mouth with the other.

Nothing is more distressing to any horse-lover than to see a heavily loaded milk or ice cart going up a steep part of the road, the horses with their heads down, straining and doing their best, and the ignorant driver lagging at their mouths. I suggest rubber bits, instead of steel bits, if drivers do not know how to drive properly.

News item, The Times, July 28. Australians will soon be offered a radically different new type of record. Decca Record Company expects to send at least 100,000 **long-playing records** to Australia in the next three months. They will also send 10,000 devices to play these records.

This presents a problem for existing record players. If the new records become popular, and all new records are of the LP type, the old players will become obsolete.

The new LP will play about five times as long as the old standard record, and can carry the whole of a symphony on a single side. It is designed to turn at 33 and a third revolutions per minute, rather than the previous 78.

With the new records, there is none of the "scratch" as with the previous type. And it will not break and shatter if dropped.

AUGUST NEWS ITEMS

It looks like a great season for Rugby League. The French team has started playing here, and the recent match at Toowoomba was full of punch-ups, kicking of players lying on the ground, and illegal head-high tackles. At one stage, the entire French team walked off for five minutes. Looks like a **typical French tour is underway**, so I won't bother you with the score in the above match….

And, as you would expect, **the Press are doing what they can to ensure that cooler heads do not prevail**. In the above match, as the Frogs were walking off, the *SMH* reported that the French captain was hit in the face by a thrown **newspaper. Can you believe in such violence? What life-threatening act will be next?**

The Minister for the Army said that boys aged 15 to 17 will be enlisted as band boys. They would be **recruited for seven and a half years.** For the first 18 months, they would be kept separate from other soldiers, and after that, posted to a Regular Army band anywhere in the nation.

King George VI is back at Buckingham palace after six weeks convalescence for catarrhal inflation of the lungs. He is described as looking well. Princess Margaret, on the other hand, **is in bed with German measles**….

Comment. These apparently trivial matters were reported on **the front page of newspapers all over Australia**. This shows the **great interest that we still had in the Royal Family**, and as a corollary, the feeling of attachment that most people still had **for Britain and the Empire**.

The NSW Government was worried about price increases for basic goods. So it introduced legislation to **freeze prices at current levels. This move was not well thought out**. In general, prices were high because there was a shortage of goods nation-wide. So, **if you were selling potatoes, say**, you would surely sell to **Victoria where the prices had been allowed to rise**, rather than to NSW where they were frozen and could not rise. So, what happened was that there were **no potatoes at all from Tasmania for NSW**, and the same was true, to an extent, for other goods.

The moral. Think before you legislate.

The NSW Chief Secretary has granted a licence to a theatrette in Kings Cross in Sydney to show cultural and religious films **on a Sunday**. A small charge will be allowed. They will be shown on a continuous basis, with five showings a day....

Churchmen objected immediately. They talked about desecrating the Sabbath, the thin edge of the wedge, difficulties in defining religious and cultural films. One Letter writer pointed out that he was a Muslim, and asked if religious films included the Muslim religion....

Comment. Of course, it was the thin edge. In sport and elsewhere, the secularisation of Sundays was slowly becoming accepted by society. And later it was demanded by society. But that would take a long time, and **the battle over the issue continued for 50 years.**

GIBBIT THE LOT

The Country Party view of Australia. The Country Party (now the Nationals) represents the farming and grazier sections of Australian politics. They were in those days, and still are, locked into an uneasy marriage with the Liberal Party as a partner which is quite unequal, but still getting some whiff of power when the Coalition wins office. This is better for them than any alternative, but they are never happy with it, because their aspirations as country-based representatives are inevitably different from those of their city-based Coalition colleagues.

In 1951, the wool boom was fading a little, but was still boosting the fortunes and morale of the country folk. So, a few of their representatives felt it was the time to give the rest of Australia a blast on all sorts of issues Below is a report of a speech, given by H Robinson, the Country Party Member for Riverina, at the opening ceremony in Sydney of the 58th Annual Conference of the Farmers and Settlers' Association. There were 130 delegates there, representing 11,500 primary producers.

Australians have become a mendicant people. That is, they are **a race of full-time beggars**. This nation, once described as one of the world's most reliant and resourceful nations, is crawling round the world market-places begging for goods and services that we are too darned lazy, or too socially stupid, to provide for ourselves.

At this very moment, we are holding out our grimy hands, stained with every kind of industrial abuse and political excess, screaming to the world "Gibbit steel. Gibbit coal. Gibbit timber. Gibbit gunyah. Gibbit ships."

We who have more coal than anyone else in the world. We who should have more and better steel, infinite quantities of timber, and illimitable capacity for house construction.

We, who have an island continent and ought to be a maritime nation, screaming to the world for ships when the floor of the seven seas is strewn with the wreckage of ships lost by other nations in our defence.

We are screaming to the war-ravaged world for people to do the jobs that we have always done, but now that we refuse to. Gibbit women to staff our institutions. Gibbit men to man our public utilities. We say that we are willing to pay for these goods and services, and that it is thus not begging. The facts are that we are only able to pay for them by the grace of God through credits built up by our primary producers. **(Much cheering and stamping of feet.)**

Not all the economic conferences, on inflation and other stuff, in Christendom will be able to change our mendicant status until there is a change of heart in the people here.

Other delegates took a similar critical stance, including the Association's General Secretary, W Scilley, who had a shot at our intention to import pre-fab houses. "It is a disgrace to our nationhood that Australia should find it necessary to call on the people of the UK, and other countries ravaged by war, to provide us with houses we are too lazy to build ourselves." He added that present Australians could only boast of their high standard of **loafing.**

FILMS TOO ON SUNDAYS

Over the past year, a number of **sporting fixtures** had been proposed for playing on Sundays. Now, State Minister Clive Evatt gave licences to a handful of theatre-owners to present movies on a Sunday. Initially, these public-spirited owners said they would only present pictures that were of high moral worth, and then only in times that did not conflict with church services. Within a few weeks, more licences were granted, and all restraints on times of presentation were gone. As you might expect, some Churches were vocal in protest. Below is a sample of their Letters on the subject.

Letters, R Cruikshank, Moderator Presbyterian Church. The granting of a licence for the opening of Sunday cinemas will cause very real alarm among the best citizens of this State.

Those most intimately in touch with the administration of NSW in recent months have every reason to view this act as the thin edge of the wedge. In the course of time, good residential districts, which now can have a hotel foisted on them against their wishes, will be in the same position with regard to Sunday places of amusement.

This is no local issue. It has national implications. In this day of destiny, when the whole human family is threatened, man needs the help of the Almighty as never before. It is a great national disservice for a Minister of the Crown to aid and abet the "Continental System" which manifestly does not promote real religion.

In our day of common peril, leaders of all sections of the community should surely take the high stand.

Letters, Alisdair Locke. I find it hard to accept implications that 50 million Britons and 150 million

Americans, at liberty to attend Sunday cinemas, are pagans and morons.

For many parents, sons and daughters, it is so often the only chance to attend the theatre en family, and for others, an opportunity to fill in the undeniably gloomier patches of what should be a happy day.

Letters, Campbell King, Secretary, Lord's Observance Society, Taree. Our Society people should weigh up the spiritual and moral decline which must follow the relaxations on the laws on Sunday pictures.

Mr Evatt must bear heavy responsibility for placing his wisdom above that committed to our trust in Holy Scripture and made part of our legislation by our forefathers, who built up Britain, not on the shifting sands of human wisdom, but on the proved revelation from above.

Letters, K McGrath. The dogmatic attitude of minority church groups on Sunday film is typical of the Church's failure to meet modern problems.

It cannot command the support and win the allegiance of large sections of the community, yet would impose its will to uphold an archaic Sunday observance law. Let the Church modernise her thinking and streamline her methods if she is to hold her own.

Letters, A Payne, President, Motion Picture Exhibitors' Association of NSW. It has been alleged that we are, behind the scenes, pushing for the general opening of theatres on Sunday. In fact, my association has expressed definite opposition to this proposal.

There are not sufficient skilled operators available for the industry to operate on a seven-day basis, and there is definite reluctance on the part of members of the Theatrical Employees' Association to work on Sundays.

Moreover, it is not economically possible for the industry to operate on a seven-day basis on our present basis.

It is the considered opinion of my association that the amount of money being spent at our box office would be spread over seven days instead of six, with the theatre being burdened by greatly increased overhead to provide Sunday entertainment. For this reason, Sunday cinemas would lead to increased prices for admission.

We are not sure, too, that the Australian public is ready to accept Sunday films. Last Sunday's screening did not help to resolve the point, with an estimated **50 per cent New Australian attendance**.

Letters, W Hilliard, Bishop Coadjutor of Sydney. You suggest that churches ought to commend the Sunday screening on the basis that "**Satan finds some mischief for idle hands to do**." However, I have yet to learn that most of the acts of delinquency are committed on Sundays. Nor have I seen any suggestion that the shows are to be confined to the teen-agers about whom you are so greatly concerned.

Moreover, it is not only idle hands that **Satan** seeks to employ. **If he can persuade** good and highly respected people to get behind a movement whose ultimate result is likely to be the secularisationof Sunday, **and** can secure the support which a great newspaper wields in the community, he will have achieved far more than by the use of certain idle adolescent hands.

Letters, S Edwards. As an ex-serviceman, I would like to ask some of the Church leaders who object to Sunday film if they object to members of the forces going into action on the Sabbath?

I have had four years active service in WWII and, with my mates, saw action on many Sundays. We tried to do our best whether it was Sunday or a week-day, and I see no reason for accepting attempted dictation as to what I can do in my own free time by way of Sunday entertainment.

These gentlemen have nothing to say about transport workers being on the job on Sunday, and I suppose that a number of church-goers use train, tram, or bus to get to the place of worship.

Letters, Belle Carlin. By all means show films on Sundays. Why not?

Let the impoverished soul, who gains nothing from quiet contemplation of the beauties of God's wonderful world; who is not stirred by the glorious harmony of cathedral of church choir, or lifted to great heights by the splendid and heart-warming message of an inspiring teacher – let him have his silver-sheet entertainment.

Letter, M Bersten. I had an occasion to reproach two New Australians (very decent types) for having indulged in wine drinking on a Sunday.

To justify themselves they took me into Pitt and George Streets, indicating the number of people aimlessly wandering the streets with nothing to do. They pleaded with me that Sunday sport and picture shows would be a lesser evil than drinking, or other immoralities, into which idle people could be drawn.

Letters, Alistair Shaw. As a young ex-Serviceman studying at present for the Presbyterian ministry, I would like to suggest that people like going to the pictures. We cannot deny that. I feel that no harm will be done on Sundays if the films shown are of such a nature that **some spiritual or moral benefit may be gained by the individuals of the audience**.

Also, that the theatre showing the films allows its audience **free admittance**. That is, the selected films must be shown not for any commercial gains but as a service to the community and to God.

Comment. The wedge **was** in. Gradually, as the influence of religion in society dropped, so Sunday trading in all spheres increased. I really do not know if this is a good thing or not. But let me say that for donkey's years, you could not buy petrol on a Sunday. Recently, I needed some Sabbath petrol, and was most relieved when I found an open service station.

KOREA YET AGAIN

This little report should really be headed "August Trivia." Or really, into a separate section called something like "August Ridiculous." There are two incidents I must include.

The first is that negotiations to establish a de-militarised zone were continuing, in the Korean large town of Kaesong, in a special area, free from combatants. At one stage in August, a platoon of North Koreans strayed into this zone, quite lost, and went out without any trouble. So that was enough for the Allies to say they were being intimidated and take their negotiators back to Tokyo for a few days. That is not the ridiculous part. It is what happened on their return. They went into conference and here is the account of the meeting.

Allied and Communist delegates re-met after the six-day break in negotiations after Communist troops violated the Kaesong neutral zone. The talks however got off to an uneasy start after the two sides **stared at each other across the table for two hours and eleven minutes, and did not exchange any words at all in this period.** Earlier there had been conversation during which time each side stated that its position had not changed. The silence was eventually broken when the American, Admiral Joy, cleared his throat and re-stated the UN position was still unchanged.

The second was a few days later. The Reds had claimed that a bomb had been dropped in the neutral zone by an American bomber. The US denied this, and broke off negotiations for four days in the time-honoured manner. When they returned to discussions, the US principal negotiator, General Ridgeway, greeted the North Koreans with this note.

Your message of August 24, pertaining to alleged incidents by elements of the UN Command, is so utterly false and so preposterous and so obviously manufactured for your own questionable purposes that it does not merit a reply in its own merit, nor do other incidents you have cited as intentional UN violations of the neutral zone at Kaesong.

When not fabricated by you for your own propaganda needs, these incidents have proven to be action by irregular groups, without the slightest connection overtly or covertly with any forces or agencies under my control.

Evidence in this most recent alleged violation was even more palpably compounded for your insidious propaganda purposes than your earlier efforts. In line with our constant adherence to the ethics of decency, I have in this case, as in all other cases, fully investigated your charges. My senior Army, Navy, and Air Force commanders have individually certified that none of their elements violated, or could possibly have violated, the Kaesong neutral zone in this or any other instance reported by you.

I have caused the results of the investigation into the most recent allegation to be widely publicised so that the entire world will be fully cognisant of your quite evident talent to use a manufactured incident in order evade your responsibility for suspending the negotiations.

Needless to say, negotiations were again broken of for a few days when this note was delivered.

Comment. I simply would not want any of the negotiators, from either side, advocating on my behalf. They aim to score petty little victories, and yet the killing goes on. On the very day that Ridgeway delivered his note, newspapers reported, for example, that "thirty-five Superfortresses dropped more than 300 tons of bombs about ten miles from the Soviet's far eastern frontier to-day when they raided ....." My point, again, is that while this mockery of peace talks was going on and on, so too was the killing of beautiful young men.

NEWS AND VIEWS

Letters, Marilyn Pitt. I am an American housewife making my home in Australia. While I appreciate the good cooking of Australian women, I am astonished at the poor standards of salads I receive in homes and cafes.

This country produces superb fruit and vegetables, which surely deserve what we call "the full treatment". They certainly don't get it. And the accompanying mayonnaises often resemble watery custard.

A well-balanced salad need not be expensive, or a nuisance to prepare, and I have found good brands of mayonnaise in the stores. But heaven spare me from what Australians euphemistically call a "salad."

Letters, C Suoden. About getting rid of pigeons. I recall, as a boy of 12, in Pyrmont, I used to ask a gentleman to get me a nip of rum for threepence, and soak wheat in it.

I laid the wheat in the school yard after school, and the pigeons would fall over drunk. I would pick them up and sell them in George Street West, near Harris Street, for a shilling each, which is better than putting poisoned wheat in the garden would be.

Margaret Truman. News item, New York. Aug 18th.

The Ford Motor Company has presented Margaret, the daughter of President Truman, with a gift of a custom-built limousine costing 28,000 dollars. It is equipped with telephone, 14-carat fittings, air-conditioning and space for a TV set. There was no special occasion for the gift.

Of course, as the daughter of the President, she is forbidden to drive. Secret Service agents do that task for her. They are restricted by law to a speed of 40 miles an hour. The car does six miles to the gallon.

Car for Margaret. News Item, London, August 18th.

Princess Margaret will turn 21 today. She will receive a Daimler car from her parents as a present. It is the first car she has owned. The King also gave her a string of pearls, for which one pearl had been set aside on each of her previous birthdays. He also gave her a pair of turquoise bracelets.

The tenants on her estate were also "happy" to contribute each a sum of two shillings to buy her an inlaid writing bureau. The King went out today for a full day of grouse shooting. The whole Royal family met up at lunch time with a picnic hamper, and toasted Margaret's health over lunch.

SEPTEMBER NEWS ITEMS

The number of **Hire Purchase agreements has risen sharply in the last three months**. The Government has asked the HP companies to do something about this, and they have responded by **raising the deposit they require** from customers. From say 10 per cent to 20 per cent....

The big increase in HP loans reflect the rising confidence of the population that the **current economic prosperity will continue**. Most of them know that HP companies charge twice the interest rate that banks do, but argue that they have the use of the goods immediately. It beats the hell out of waiting till they have the money in hand. **"Buy now, Pay later" say the ads.**

A Catholic priest in Melbourne had just finished saying Mass when a woman accosted him with a rifle and **shot him in the arm**. Police indicate that **the woman is a "religious fanatic"** and that she is likely to attack again. A Catholic men's group, the Holy Names Society, will form **a barrier around the church in St Kilda** for Sunday's Mass tomorrow.

The NSW Rugby League has decided that it will **play this year's Grand Final at the Sydney Cricket Ground.** The crowd is expected to be the normal 60,000 people....

The choice of ground is not surprising because **the final has been played there for years**. But the date is a bit startling. It had been **changed from the traditional Saturday to a Sunday. And of course, patrons will**

pay to enter. Some people are not happy. Another challenge, the biggest yet, to the sanctity of Sundays.

Apprehension is growing over the health of the King. This morning he visited a specialist, and his chest was the subject of his visit. The Palace will not reveal information, but there is a sombre feeling that his illnesses have persisted and **something serious is amiss. In late September, he got even sicker.**

Some **miners in the western NSW coalfields** went on strike yesterday because of **the shortage of butter.** The Central **Committee of the Miners' Federation** said that their action was "**completely justified and understandable.**"

Towards the end of August**, the Federal Treasurer brought down a tough budget.** Drinkers and smokers were hard hit, income tax was increased by 10 per cent, and sales taxes increases of the order of five per cent were introduced....

Menzies and Treasurer Fadden said the idea was to remove money from circulation and **thus reduce inflation**. Inflation was indeed a bugbear for everyone. So while everyone resented the new strictures, they more or less saw them as reducing the inflation menace....

Menzies did not say was that **the extra revenue he got would be used to pay for the unpopular war in Korea**. This war was getting more unpopular by the day, **so Menzies avoided saying that it had to be paid for. How? By higher taxes.**

Economists and newspapers were very critical of the budget. They argued that despite Fadden's assurances, the new taxes on everything **would add to, and not reduce, inflation**. They argued that a company **tax rate of 50 per cent** would cripple industry. They argued that his promise of a surplus would not happen because **wool and commodity prices had just taken a nose-dive.**

Comment. Menzies ruled by simple formulae that he applied time after time. He **had just been returned to power** with control of the Senate to boot. His formula at this point was **to bring down an unpopular budget**, and as new elections approached, gradually loosen the purse strings and then before the next election, **present a very popular budget. Seems simple, but he retired after 16 years, the undefeated champion.**

A labourer on a work site in Sydney was arrested and gaoled for three days. He was charged with **deserting from the Air Force**. He was flown to Brisbane, and appeared before the Court. There, it turned out that he **had never been in the Air Force,** and he was freed. He said that he had protested throughout his innocence. **He intends to sue the Air Force.**

Stay away from Bankstown, a Sydney suburb. **563 detonators were stolen** from a quarry, and have not been traced. Each of them looks like a fountain pen, and if it explodes**, it could cause the death of a group of children. If you sight them, please contact Bankstown Police.**

Once again, the land is being **devastated by bushfires**. The Minister for Conservation in NSW delivered a "shocking report." In it, he said that some of the fires were started by fire-bugs. We already knew that. He went on to say that another major cause was part-time firefighters who **deliberately started fires so that they could be paid for putting them out.** Another lurk was to light fires on the job, so as to earn over-time....

He also told of forest leaseholders who set fires to burn out low-lying scrub. This enables **grazing on the denuded land. He wants gaol, without the option of a fine, for offenders.**

Police in Melbourne's St Kilda are **stopping people leaving the beach in their swimming costumes.** They are saying that both women and men must cover up from shoulder to thigh. This was because there have been complaints about women in two-piece suits and men in very brief trunks parading to the shops near the beach.

Comment. What will happen when the bikini comes in full swing in a few years?

Crocodiles apparently like music, according to some professional hunters. They report that **they come to the surface and cruise** when music is played on a portable gramophone. At the moment, it is thought that **they appreciate boogie and Bach equally**, but more research needs to be done on this.

Tattooing studios in Sydney, already badly effected by rationing, are complaining that **their businesses are being severely damaged by the blackouts.**

MENZIES SHOT DOWN

Robert Gordon Menzies had been busy over the last few months. He had held a big national convention that looked at the problem of inflation. He had made many statements that said we were in danger of being attacked by various hues of Reds, and we had to tighten our belts to pay for our defence and also to curb inflation. And, now, he continued his attacks on local Reds with a referendum to be held on September 22nd.

The issue for decision was a familiar one. He wanted to change the Constitution so that he could close down the Communist Party, and confiscate its property. And he wanted power to "declare" Reds as such, and thereby ensure that they were not employed by any form of Government, and that they would be stigmatised throughout society. So, he put it to the people via the ballot box.

By now, readers will be familiar with the issues involved here, and I will only give a few glimpses of some quirky aspects of the campaign.

Letters, Rev G Julian, Murrumburrah-Harden. It is quite obvious that there is a strange coalition making a mighty endeavour to force through a piecemeal alteration to the Constitution, which, in spite of the naive protests that such a thing could not happen, could easily be turned to account by a non-paternal government.

I will vote "NO", not because I underestimate the Communist menace, nor because I have any sympathy with Communism, but because I will not tolerate the Australian Constitution becoming a modern form of the Inquisition, which is still dear to the totalitarian heart.

The success of the "YES" vote would create a new power. This would be a centralised power; an unrestricted power over the personal liberty of Australians; a power dearly loved by totalitarians, whether secular or religious.

The issue of the referendum has been confused by charges of Communism, hysteria, and sectarianism, levelled against those who have a right to say why they object to this attempt to tamper with the Constitution; and by the advocates of the "YES" vote in their attempt to trade Communism for Fascism.

Letters, D Walsh. Dr Soper, the visiting evangelist, is reported as having said "If you are going to get rid of Communism, you will have to do it with Christian methods, and not Communist methods."

By all means let us use Christian methods. Let us refer to the Bible and cast them out with much force and violence, just as Christ did to the money-changers in the temple.

Letters, C Chapman. The whole of Christ's teaching is based on love, not hate. I agree with Dr Soper that we cannot maintain our moral superiority if we threaten local Communists with political repression and international ones with the atom bomb.

Letters, J Leslie. During the week-end I saw the callous defacement of property by the painting of unsightly and indelible "NO" on house walls and sacrosanct places such as the noble gate-columns of Centennial Park.

This has tipped the scales for me. If this is the democracy that is being saved for us by the advocates of the "NO" vote, I wish to be spared from it. I could never believe that any Party which permits things like this could genuinely stand for the liberty of the subject. I shall take a chance on giving the Government too much power.

Both Party leaders spent lots of time on the hustings addressing public meetings. Menzies, with a mixture of arrogance and humour, fought his way through much heckling and cat-calling to meet abuse with abuse. "I have to deal with scum like you all the time". "It is a great pity that some of the young men and women here don't go right off to Russia." "As for gangs like you, you know I despise you. If I had my way, you would not be saying boo. You'd be saying boo-hoo."

Dr Evatt, as Leader of the Opposition, was more stolid, and less challenging. But he hammered away at the basics. "Anyone can be defined as a Communist, then declared, slandered and deprived of property and civil rights." "This is sheer and utter totalitarianism of the Right. In other words, Fascism." "Menzies promised he would put value back into the Pound. Why then is he convening giant conferences on the terrible effects of inflation? Why does he not encourage people to work more instead of putting back controls that were dropped four years ago?"

So the nation went to the polls on that Saturday. No one was sure who would win. At the close of counting on the Saturday night, the results seemed to be a good win for the Liberals and Bob Menzies. But later counting indicated that he lost by a very small margin.

Mr Menzies vowed that he would keep fighting; which he did. Evatt said that Menzies should now resign; which he did not. The battle against the Reds had to be fought in other ways.

A short note on Korea. After Ridgeway's note to the Reds, meetings between the two sides were cancelled for a month. In that period, Admiral Nam, the chief Red, wrote a dirty note back to Ridgeway. **He too was full of the conciliation that was customary.** "You are trying to escape from your side's inescapable responsibility for the Kaesong neutrality violations and for obstructing the process of the armistice negotiations. We consider your letter completely unsatisfactory and unacceptable." So things just got murkier, and of course, there were still no serious attempts at talks.

Then the Americans insisted that Kaesong was not a proper place to have these meetings. They argued that "the Kaesong neutral zone is but a few minutes from the most important supply line in your rear area. Thousands of aircraft sorties are directed against this line of supply. The likelihood of an accidental occurrence involving Kaesong is inevitable". This half-hearted admission of complicity, however, won no friends, and the North Koreans refused to budge. So, September ended with no talks in sight.

Meanwhile the death toll kept mounting. Here is a quote from a US Lieutenant Colonel, **on a typical day**, "The Communists suffered at least 400 dead, and 1,600 casualties. We got all our men out, the living, the wounded and the dead. We left dead Chinese all piled up like cordwood. The Chinese used the damnedest artillery and mortar barrage that I know of. It turned the place black with shell craters."

Comment. This war is getting me down. I will not report on it again till December if all that happens is just a repeat of the hopelessness of the last few months.

MARGARINE IN THE NEWS

News item, September 21ˢᵗ. Margarine. The Country Party Member for Byron said in the Legislative Assembly that the **NSW whaling industry** posed a threat to the butter producers of the State. With butter so expensive, margarine was becoming a viable alternative, and much more of it was being used for home consumption.

Margarine can be made from whale oil, and he foresaw the production of whale oil becoming so large that butter sales would suffer. He pointed out that a company called Whale Industry Limited aimed at catching 500 humpback whales per year, extracting seven tons of oil from each, and using the oil for production of margarine. It could also be used for pharmaceutical products and for nitroglycerine. Given the fact that many European nations were now ready to export butter, this was a threat that dairy farmers could not take lightly.

Letters, Phillip Caro. As Chief Messing Officer to the AIF in England in WWI, I instituted the making of margarine in our camps. The process was simple, and the product first class.

For those people who have a supply of beef fat and milk, here is the recipe.

Dripping 4 pounds, milk one pint, salt one ounce, butter colour one-fifth ounce. First sour the milk and beat up until all clots are broken and quite liquid. Pour the dripping (heated to 100 degrees F) into it and beat up vigorously. Add the salt and colour, and beat up in a tin container, surrounded by cold water, until it sets, and then pour it into cold water and allow it to remain there until it sets up. Leave it to set up properly for 12 hours.

When the margarine is made, it is quite easy to mix half margarine and butter, so as to obtain a good product which passes easily for butter.

QUESTIONS OF LOYALTY TO BRITAIN

Letters, G Bennett-Wood, Secretary, UK Services' Association. The Agent General to NSW has said that Australia should not sell meat to Britain unless she receives "very favourable prices." He knows, he says, that Norway, Sweden, and other countries are anxious to buy Australian meat.

In short, the Australian representatives in London are holding a pistol at Britain's head and saying, in effect, "Pay our prices or starve."

Britain, as we know, threw everything she had into the last war while some other nations, at first anyway, stood aloof and took a hell-sent opportunity for filling their pockets. Now she is faced with an enormous rearmament problem.

No doubt we can take advantage of Britain's present dilemma to secure very favourable prices indeed for our primary products. We can, in short, weaken Britain's economy and keep her people hungrier than they need to be, for the sake of a few extra millions which will eventually serve to inflate our top-heavy economy. But we cannot do this and keep our self-respect.

Letters, W Kellie. As a British ex-Serviceman I would like to point out that, through the waste of the Socialist Government, the UK is now unable or unwilling to pay a reasonable price for her meat.

This Government was able to throw 36 million Pounds down the drain for their "ground nut scheme." And a further million for the "Gambia egg scheme."

It is about time Australia and the rest of the Dominions refused to allow themselves, through loyalty, to be **mulcted** of just prices.

Letters, E Ogilvie. Why do Australians have to send a Minister for Agriculture abroad to sell our produce, in this case our meat, which half the world is clamouring for at remunerative prices?

If Governments have to take over our produce, should not negotiations for sale be held in Australia? In London, Mr McEwen will be surrounded by all the skill of Old World diplomacy. The dominating influence will be political.

The fact that low export prices have closed down so many cattle stations, once producing for export, seems to be of no importance to the paid negotiator, whose one object is price reduction for political purposes, regardless of its effect on the land.

Comment. The Agent General's attitude, backed up by Mr Kellie, that we should sell to the highest bidder is now self-evident. But not in 1951. It was a new concept. For the War-years, Britain's needs became Australia's needs, and our nation was very conscious of all the problems that Britain faced. Witness, for example, the Food for Britain campaign that had sent enormous quantities of gifts of food to that nation from private citizens, and which had just finished in 1950. There was still a dominant belief here that we were part of the British Empire, and that meant making sacrifices in real terms for the Brits.

But the Agent General, and Mr Kellie, did not agree. They wanted a commercial price. Then Mr Ogilvie also introduced a new concept. **Why not have buyers come here?** Again, this was a break with long-standing tradition, and **a symbolic statement that we were learning to stand up for ourselves**. If you look ahead a few years when members of the Royal family visited Australia, and you see the rapturous reception they universally got, you realise that our ties to Britain were still extremely strong.

Nevertheless, every now and then, small indications of national independence kept popping up with increasing frequency until now in 2019, of course, we are just about free from British influence, even to the extent of perhaps cutting our ties to the monarchy.

FOUR QUESTIONS AND THREE ANSWERS

A reader is not happy with the philosophy of the government's budget changes. He poses a few questions .

Question One: You are a Government whose electoral mandate may fairly be summarised as **destroying Communism, removing controls, and reducing taxation.**

You have had neither the legal acumen to devise symbols of action against Communism within the Constitution, nor the political energy or ability to convince the electorate that a constitutional amendment is necessary. So you won't be destroying Communism.

In these circumstances what do you do about items (b) and (c) of your mandate? **The answer**, clearly, is that you should go ahead and impose blanket controls, and double taxation. You simply have no choice.

Question Two: You are a Prime Minister whose Government is submitting **a record** peacetime Budget. The Budget has been prepared by economic advisers who have spared you, your Treasurer, and themselves, the trouble of thinking. Softening the public for doom to come, you have stressed defence preparations as the cause of extra expenditure. You have told us about many wars that might blow up in our face, and we will have to fight them. How much of your revenue should go to defence – 50 per cent, 60 per cent, or some larger amount?

The answer is a maximum of 15 per cent. This might shock everyone in the nation, including your own Party, but it is nice to hope that all those wars have suddenly gone away.

Question Three: You are a rank-and-file Parliamentary supporter of the Government mentioned in Question One. You have honestly expounded at two elections what you have honestly believed to be its policy. Now you find yourself confronted with the Federal Budget of September, 1951. Now there are taxes where there were none before, and everything is miles more expensive. You are not prepared to fight the matter out at party meetings while it is still technically possible to amend the Budget. What is your course of action?

Answer: Sit tight; shut up; **hope that the ravens will feed you**; and spend your spare time learning some useful craft or occupation which may be an income-earner after the next election.

Question Four: You are an elector who does not belong to a political party. You discarded Labour in 1949 because of its deference to bureaucracy, its love of controls, and its certainty that it could do better with money you really needed than you could yourself. You have on your hands the Menzies Government of 1951. What do you do now? (NOTE: Suicide and blasphemy are not acceptable answers to this question.)

Answer: There is no acceptable answer to this question.

NEWS AND VIEWS

Letters, BANDSMAN. Thousands of bandsmen and band-lovers will, no doubt, be amazed at the announcement that **the ABC is to dispense with its military band.**

This combination, the only one of its kind in Australian radio, selects its programmes to satisfy all tastes and presents them musically and tunefully. It has not only been a source of enjoyment to many thousands of people, but has also been a guide to the many amateur brass bands in existence.

Letters, Peter Nelson. The dismissal of the ABC Military band for reasons of economy will not unduly perturb radio listeners. Limited in scope and listening appeal, and non-revenue-producing, the band has occupied too long valuable space on a National program whose aims are supposedly educational and aesthetic.

A DRUG PROBLEM

News item, September 23rd.   Three raids were made by Customs Officers on opium dens in Dixon Street, Sydney last night. Several Chinese were charged with having prohibited opium in their possession. The raids yielded three Pounds of opium, the largest amount seized for some time.

Fifty six smokers were found in the premises, and records seized indicated that large quantities of the drug were regularly traded. The opium was selling for ten Shillings per smoke.

OCTOBER NEWS ITEMS

The first Australian Golf Open held in Melbourne this week. It was won by professional Peter Thompson. He had been a promising amateur as a young man, then went out of the limelight for two years while he gained his professional qualification. He now won the first Open by one shot from fiery Norman von Vida....

Comment. I have seen many young sportsmen do well in one event, and then fade into oblivion. I expect that Thompson will do just that, and **we will never hear from him again.**

The Royal Tour by the King and Queen has been cancelled, because the King has had a lung removed. This tour was scheduled for March next year, and **Princess Elizabeth and Prince Phillip will tour in their stead**. Princess Margaret will no longer make the trip as had been originally planned.

A week after the announcement of the impending visit by Elizabeth, **dozens of provincial cities have applied** to State Directors of the tour **to have their cities included for Royal visits.** They made different arguments supporting their requests, but **all of them promised that all children within a 10-mile radius would be shipped in to provide the cheering masses.**

There have been a number of qualified medical practitioners who have said **that cancer can be caused by a virus**, and that it **can be spread from person to person**, rather like the flu....

The theory has gained credence since it was announced that **well-known and respected philanthropist, Sir Edward Hallstrom, is financing experiments** to check its validity. **Responsible medical authorities in this nation are all cautiously rejecting the theory.**

The Prime Minister of Australia is now a grandfather for the first time.

Britain has a new Prime Minister, a bloke called Winston Churchill. He replaces the former Labour Prime Minister, Clement Atlee. One of Labour's weaknesses was that it wanted to nationalise private enterprises, at a time when Britain generally **wanted to be free from the sort of controls that came with socialism**....

Very few voters still saw Churchill as the godlike figure that he had been during the War, but **his lack of coherent policies** was preferred by the majority over the **structured society that Atlee espoused.** Australia's Labor Party should take note.

Melbourne had been selected as the site for the 1956 Olympic Games. But the Premier of Victoria said that Victoria was not prepared to **arrest the development of housing** and education or like, just so **that it could pay for the Olympics**....

So, after the euphoria of the choice of Melbourne, the hard **reality of financing the Games** came to the fore and the **many years of squabbling with the Federal Government** started.

MAINLY RURAL MATTERS

Australia's Aborigines were a topic that was not at the forefront of public discussion. Every white person in the community had strong views on matters Aboriginal, and they were quite willing to tell you all about them, for or against, but **privately**, at the drop of a hat. But, as was also true for sex, **public** discussion was muted and careful. So it was all the more surprising when a letter from Mr Sawtell appeared, and then the many co-respondents joined in.

Michael Sawtell was a member of the NSW Aborigines Board. Following from a comment from a Government official, he acknowledged that some Aborigines did live under what seemed to be deplorable conditions, but he suggested that they might not find them so bad. "They might prefer to live that way." He goes on to ask whether we are justified in forcing our way of living on to them if they do not want to change.

He pointed out that his Board had spent a lot of money to build houses for the Aborigines, but now it was having great difficulty in getting back even the smallest of rental payments. There is nothing now to prevent the humblest aboriginal in this State from becoming a highly useful and respected citizen, if he cares to make the effort, but very few of them care to do so.

He went on to say that if any Aborigine wanted to become a citizen on equal standing with the whites, there was nothing to stop him. But he added that if that led to detribalisation, it would cause enormous problems for these wonderful people in their own natural habitat.

"There is much sentimental nonsense talked about their welfare, and in the N.T. the Federal Government is spoiling many good stock boys. Most aborigines do not want, understand, or appreciate what we are trying to do for them."

Sawtell's letter got many pens scratching

Letters, Kenneth Jones, Dean, Armidale. Mr Sawtell surprises me. He says that some aborigines might prefer to live in deplorable conditions. Perhaps he might like to tell that to the local aborigines round this area.

He thinks there is nothing to stop the humblest aborigine in the State from becoming respectable, if he cares to make the effort. It might interest him to know that whether there is any theoretical or legal bar to them so doing, there is a very strong prejudice against coloured folk entering some of the professions, such as nursing. **Or even being treated in hospitals.** And this prejudice factor is one of the greatest bars to their entering upon full citizenship and being absorbed into the life of the community.

What we are doing is not only taking their land, but de-tribalising because in that land was impressed those tribal associations that go with the tribal spirit. The whites inexorably keep on, and the aborigines must take their chance. If they cannot live with it, then they just die. Have a read of the book "Water into Gold."

Letters, G Fisher, The Armidale School. Mr Sawtell's letter on conditions of aborigines contains several half-truths which are probably not intended to do harm to the cause of the kindly 60,000 who are still denizens but not citizens of Australia.

No one who has seen Aborigines in their own haunts over the years would deny that many are not sufficiently advanced to take advantage of the white people's amenities. At present, the majority are suffering from all the disadvantages that Mr Sawtell rightly calls "deplorable".

Included among these are T.B. and V.D. and others, a lack of suitable housing facilities, forms of segregation in schooling and housing, etc. But worst of all is the deprivation of civic rights from all who have more than 50 per cent of "black" blood. All of these pay their taxes, but can not vote. Surely we can grant social security benefits to those who are not getting maternity allowances, and other benefits.

Mr Sawtell got out of all that without too much criticism. So, apparently, he decided to write again, and came up with perhaps a more provocative letter.

Letters, Michael Sawtell. Many of those aborigines who live on the banks of creeks do so because they **have easier access to liquor and the women are able to practise prostitution**. All of these people are now on the basic wage of ten Pounds per week, and they hire taxis to take them to and from the nearest town. The Board is no more able to force them to be good citizens than **the clergy are able to force white people to become good Christians**.

The hard irrefutable facts are **that civilisation in all its forms spells the doom of our aborigines**. The missionaries do much good work. They also do much harm when they try to convert the aborigines to Christianity. When you destroy a man's native faith, you must demoralise a man.

Last year in NSW, the Board spent 200,000 Pounds on aboriginal welfare. Many of the so-called aborigines in this State are nearly white. In fact, we may be now trying to do too much for our aborigines.

Letters. Colin Simpson. When Mr Sawtell says that too much is being done for aborigines, he is talking the sort of defeatist nonsense which does these fine people the greatest sort of injustice.

They are still, for instance, receiving third-rate education, mainly through missions who do on the cheap the job that should be done adequately by State education authorities.

I think it will be found that Albert Namatjira's alleged "refusal to take up responsibilities for citizenship" is due to the fact that he has received such a poor education that he stills finds it difficult to write an adequate letter of application.

Letters, Grac. The derisive reference to the missions "doing things on the cheap" is unfair. The achievements of any human enterprise cannot be measured by its cost. Splendid work is being done by these people (mainly women), in the face of heavy odds, in hostels and institutes conducted for the sole benefit of aborigines and half-bloods. The Flying Doctor Service was inaugurated by one such Mission. Also the Channel Island leprosarium near Darwin and at Townsville.

It is not by cynicism and reproach but by wise, compassionate action that the difficulties of absorbing these descendents of an ancient race into a modern society can be attacked.

Mr Sawtell was not daunted by these objections.

Letters, Michael Sawtell. On any mission station, you will see thoroughly domesticated young aboriginal women, who are able to read and write, are interested in women's fashions, and who help to translate the Bible into their own dialect.

Now, who are these girls to marry? The missionaries hope that these girls will make Christian marriages with full-blood boys, but those girls do not, for there is always a tendency for educated and sophisticated aborigines to look for mates among people of a lighter caste. Those girls now hope to marry white or half-caste boys. Likewise, half-caste girls hope to marry any kind of white man.

It is utterly impossible to de-tribalise and Christianise our full-blood aborigines without causing great cruelty and social damage. Aboriginal welfare is a very difficult and complicated process.

Comment. The various writers, all with the best of intentions, scarcely came together long enough to argue a single point. It just gives an idea of how far debate on aboriginal matters had yet to go.

KANGAROOS

In a lengthy Letter, Mr Mendel of Mosman, in Sydney, said there were very few kangaroos in the outback, and that reports of damage caused by them was a gross exaggeration. In the Letters below, he was first politely corrected, and then other Letters made it clear that the roos were very much a matter of interest to the Outback.

Letters, G.I.H. Mr A Mendel states that he saw only 38 kangaroos on a trip of 900 miles. I have shot hundreds of kangaroos over 40 years, and know their habits. They get on the move before dusk and go into camp soon after sunrise and it is surprising your correspondent saw even 38. One thing they do is keep clear of roads where there is traffic.

Letters, J Dyer. In reply to Mr Mendel, let me say that I live, travel and work in the Dubbo, Warren, Carinda and Macquarie Marsh districts, and have only two weeks ago seen a mob of 200 kangaroos or more running across open plain country.

Also, I know of a landholder who paid 300 Pounds per mile to have a fence constructed adjoining a State

Forest only to find that kangaroos had broken the netting in no less than 11 places four weeks after its construction.

Incidentally, kangaroos do not come near roads frequented by motor traffic during daylight if they can help it.

Letters, H Mallard. The Chief Secretary has seen a sinister significance in the fact that farmers usually ask for permission to reduce the numbers of kangaroos on their properties when kangaroo skins have a good market value. He says that they are only interested in getting money for the skins, and not in any serious attempt to reduce the menace on their properties.

If he were better acquainted with the farmers' circumstances, he would realise that his suspicions were unfounded. The average farmer is not equipped to deal with kangaroos. He usually depends on professional shooters, who have both the equipment and the experience to do the job.

Professionals shoot for the market, and naturally select the time of the year when the quality of skins is at its best. The farmer would not be able to enlist their help in ridding him of a major pest without this inducement. Farmers seek permission only when they can get a contract with a shooter.

The US manufacturers will take as many kangaroo skins as this country will supply, so why leave the skins to rot on the ground when this country needs dollars so badly?

Letters, Miss Ruth Schleicher. Your Letters talk about the menace to pastures. In view of the fact that kangaroos rear normally but one young once a year, and many of these fall victims to dingoes and eagles, how can they increase so rapidly as to reach plague proportions. To me, it does not seem to make sense.

If kangaroos are really doing so much damage, surely personal investigations by the Chief Guardian of Fauna would be welcomed by pastoralists. Seeing the just reason for their complaints, he could then give authoritative information to the Minister, who would act accordingly.

But unfortunately, only too often in the past, the desire for gain has brought our wild-life to near, if not complete, extinction. Therefore, a thorough sifting of evidence is justified, especially during the breeding season, when the killing of female kangaroos means a double tragedy also in the death of the young.

Letters, W Young, Condobolin. Roos are a menace, particularly to wheat crops. The big and mature ones hop over the top, or they hit the top wires and break them The half-grown and younger ones clamber over, or try to climb over, and tear the netting or break it away. If you do not see the break within 24 hours, the rabbits are in your wheat crop.

No amount of tear-jerking sophistry and "let's all be reasonable" Letters can change the fact. If we don't get the kangaroos, they will get us. Without wheat and wool, we might as well hand the land back to the aborigines.

RABBITS GALORE

Continuing with the rural theme, I am looking at a 1951 recipe for Baked Rabbit Fondu. **It starts with the item "one rabbit."** It might surprise a few readers to know that it is still easy to buy rabbits now-a-days in the year 2016. If your butchers don't have them in stock, they will get some for you the next day. Of course, they will not be the real thing. The rabbits today are carefully grown in special farms, are nice and fat, and have big succulent legs, and even have some meat on their ribs. But **the real rabbits of 1951** were scrawny, often with a bullet hole in them or with only three good legs, and with no semblance of meat anywhere near their ribs. They were, to say the least, rangy.

OUR TRADE WITH JAPAN

There were very few people who were prepared to forgive and forget the Japanese. Still, there were some among us who did. The Letter below reflects the developing tensions over this issue.

Letters, Phillip Saunders, Tokyo. I am an Australian businessman resident in Tokyo for the past five years promoting general trade between Australia and Japan. In view of WWII, the natural prejudice that is still strong in Australia against Japanese products is understandable.

But what is not so logical, judging from recent reports in the Australian Press, is how Australians can allow such prejudice to adversely affect their economy, good name, personal comfort, and standard of living.

A director of a London house of exporters is quoted as saying "This is one of about 500 British firms buying Japanese goods, and exporting them to Empire markets.... British firms who place Japanese goods in Empire markets are expecting business to surge."

That means that Australia is buying Japanese goods from the UK at perhaps three times the same goods could be brought direct form Japan.

The Federal Secretary of the Clothing Trades Union in Melbourne, Mr E Smith, is quoted as saying "We will fight to the last man and woman to stop cheap Japanese clothing coming into Australia."

Are we to understand that Mr Smith does not want Australian people to have good, cheap clothing, and will fight to the last man and woman unionist to keep prices up?

NEWS AND VIEWS

Letters, M Rathbone. Although no invitation has been received, it seems that the Sydney Symphony Orchestra will be sent en masse to the Edinburgh Music Festival next year. The cost will probably be round about 50,000 Pounds and the bill will be footed by the taxpayer.

The necessity for a complete orchestra to travel 12,000 miles just to play a few selections is doubtful, especially when recordings of the same group could be forwarded, and could be broadcast in England.

This seems a fitting occasion to point out that the RSPCA cannot obtain more than 500 Pounds per year from the State Labour Government to carry on the good work of ridding this city of starving cats and dogs. This work has increased since the meat shortage, and the position is almost out of hand. Surely the public funds can be expended in a better way than at present.

Letters, SCHOOLBOY TRAVELLER. A fine of 10 Pounds is to be imposed on persons breaking bus queues. But there are some picking-up places where, unless better arrangements are made, it will scarcely be possible to obey the regulation.

When 10 or 20 passengers are queued there is no alternative but to break the queue to catch one's particular bus as it pulls in. It often happens that two buses, sometimes three, come at the same moment.

Mailing Tea. Letters, R Blayney. Having had occasion to send a half-pound of tea to England along with other articles, I made up a parcel sewn in calico and took it to the Post Office. A form was filled in stating the contents of the parcel, but being an honest fool, I mentioned the half-pound of tea. I was informed that no tea was exported without a special permit. I tramped to No. 52

Clarence Street, the Tea and Coffee control Board, paid one shilling and threepence, and got a permit.

The Tea Control Board then stated I must go to the Customs House to get the permit stamped. The obvious remedy is to pay the money direct to the Post Office and then add a special duty stamp.

Dorothy Hart was in the news in Hollywood for the reason that she had been picked to become **Tarzan's sixteenth lady**. RKO had chosen her to play opposite Lex Barker in *"Tarzan the Hunted"*. This would have been a movie about the jungle, and monkeys, and might even have had a young lad in it called Sabu, or something similar.

Of course, **the real Tarzan** was Johnny Weismuller. He had undoubtedly crunched more villains in pith helmets than any man in history. As a young man, **he had represented the US at the Olympics in swimming**, and went on to make 10 Tarzan movies. He had been pensioned off from the role a couple of years earlier. His famous lines "**UUHHH Me Tarzan**" remain one of the classics of modern drama, both for their content and the impeccable yet imaginative delivery.

Letters, W Rowe. Why not try out the idea of giving tram and bus conductors a small percentage of their daily gross takings. As each man paid in his bag, he would be given a commission on his earnings.

I feel sure that the departmental receipts would leap high and instead of avoiding passengers, conductors would queue for peak hour shifts.

NOVEMBER NEWS ITEMS

The great potato fiasco drags on. Remember that NSW froze some basic commodity prices, including potatoes. So that sellers from interstate would not sell there. That meant a scarcity. **Now,** potatoes in NSW are so scarce that interstate growers are **keen to sell there, but not though the fixed price set by the Potato Board.** That is, by selling direct to the retailers, at the high price that householders will pay if the price freeze is ignored....

So, now **growers in Queensland are being prosecuted for selling direct to NSW retailers.** They are pretty cross, because they have surplus stock, and NSW has a famine, and never the twain can legally meet.

Control Boards across the nation are held to be pains in the neck. During the war, they proliferated, and their powers became legendary. When the war finished, they were loath to give up their powers, and in 1951 **they were clinging against all logic to their exalted position.** There were wheat Boards, egg Boards, various grain Boards, and Boards for milk, coal and what have you....

They were supposed to be mediators between capital and labour, and to keep their industry running smoothly, by managing disputes. In some cases, on some occasions, they did this, **but in general they were seen to be tools of government, or so self-interested** as to be worse than useless. In the case of the Potato Board, the folly of the NSW State Government, with the acquiescence of the Board, ensured that once again the interference of Boards would be seen **as incompetence and poor decisions making**.

Princess Elizabeth could not make her much-anticipated tour of Canada and the US because of her father's illness. **So Princess Margaret went instead.** She was much feted all the way. At a reception hosted by the President, Truman proclaimed "As I little boy, I read about **a fairy princess**." Turning to Margaret, he added "and there she is." He went on to say "My wife Margaret tells me that whenever anyone becomes acquainted with you, **they immediately fall in love with you. I believe it**."

The cricket world was agog. The West Indies team was here and about to start a Test series against Australia. The three W's, Worrell, Weekes and Walcott were set to play havoc among their white opponents. When the Poms came here a few years ago, the Press were ready to denounce them for every odd incident. But **with the Windies, there were no signs of rancour, just big grinning images** and excessive politeness.

Prices have been rising at a frantic pace. At a time of inflation and the wage-prices spiral, all the normal items like meat and vegetable have gone up ten per cent. Other things, not so conspicuous, have risen as mush. For example, **tickets to the movies, haircuts, and shoe repairs**. **But the grand daddy of all rises** was announced in mid-November with the **36 per cent increase in household gas prices** for Sydney.

MENACE OF INFLATION

November, thankfully, was a quieter month. There were no major overseas stories, no great calamities, no political eruptions. Just life as usual, except that it was so quiet as to be unusual.

On the home front, the major topic was inflation. The wages-inflation spiral, that we got so accustomed to later on, was just really beginning, and was causing much consternation. Housewives across the nation were asking what was the point of getting wage increases when the cost of everything was going up just as fast. There was no doubt prices were galloping. For example, in one night in Canberra, and a fairly typical night at that, the price that farmers got for their wheat for stock food was increased from eight to sixteen shillings a bushel. Good for them, you might say. But that meant that the prices of eggs, pork, bacon, ham and milk went up at the same time. Not too much gain here for the average household. The increase in the recent price of meat was about thirty per cent..

Letters, Bruce Rainford. Senator O'Byrne has asked the Government to issue a five Shilling note, but I may suggest that what is really needed is a two Pound note. Currency depreciation and mounting costs obviate the necessity of a five Shilling note.

The same arguments can be applied to Mr Hancock's suggestion for a four penny coin, called "the groat" for some wonderful reason, instead of our penny and three-pence. Certainly this coin would buy a one-section bus or tram ticket right now. But for how long would trade-union demands allow the fare to remain at this figure.

One-man buses. In most of the major cities, there was talk about introducing single-decker one-man buses to replace double-deckers. The Unions' arguments against these were that the driver had enough to do to in driving, and further that he would be very vulnerable to attack all by himself. The owners of buses, normally the State Governments, said that having two persons man a single-decker bus was too expensive, and this was causing fare increases.

This was a battle that was just starting. For a long time, the compromise in most areas was to have a single-decker with two men aboard, and clearly this did little to cut costs. A later development, now twenty or more years down the track, was to have a single driver on a single-decker, but to open only the front door. This was before ticketing machines were introduced, and they caused great hassles at the entrance, and great scrambles for people at the back of the bus when it came time to get off. But, now fifty years later, it all seems to have worked out OK.

Interesting, isn't it, to look back on it and think how long it takes to get solutions to social problems. In this case, the many differing groups inside Government and the many groups inside the Unions had to come to terms. But equally, so too did society as a whole, and I suspect that society is at times slower to accept change than the protagonists.

The 40-hour week. While I am loitering near the industrial front, let me point to a small but noticeable group of people who were agitating for a move away from the 40-hour week. This had been introduced in different Awards to different Unions about four years ago, and marked a reduction in the hours generally worked per week, down from the 44 or 48 previously worked. At the time it was introduced, generally over the dead bodies of employers, it was argued that, because everyone would be working fewer hours, but would still be getting paid the same, prices and inflation would inevitably rise.

Now that inflation had risen, there were quite a few who blamed it all on the 40-hour week. They were only a little bit right, because this inflation, like all of our post-War inflations, was directly imported from overseas. But they persisted, and nagged away, off and on, at those who felt and hoped that the reduced hours were here for all time.

Letters, J Peel. Surely our politicians must realise the mess the country has drifted into since the introduction of the 40-hour week.

Most State enterprises appear to be going bankrupt, foodstuffs are getting scarcer and dearer, and if the rot is not soon halted, there will be very little food for ourselves. And certainly none to export.

What with the 40-hour week coaxing large numbers of good men off the land, and high taxation, the incentive for the man on the land to boost production has been taken away. The rates on my farm before the 40-hour week was introduced were 240 Pounds. This year, I paid 735 Pounds.

CALL TO THE NATION

On November 12, the leaders of the Churches and of the Judiciary in Australia combined together to issue a **Call to all Australians** to behave in ethical and moral ways, and to beware the dangers that would befall us if we did not. This most unusual event was delivered to the public, by a statement to the newspapers, through the Chief Justice of

Victoria, Sir Edmund Herring, and came with the signatures of 100 leading Church and legal figures, as well as business and civic leaders.

It started with: "A call to the people of Australia. There are times in the histories of peoples when those charged with high responsibilities should plainly speak their minds.

"Australia is in great danger from abroad. We are in danger at home. We are in danger from moral and intellectual apathy, from the mortal enemies of mankind which sap the will and darken the understanding and breed evil dissensions....."

The document went on to enumerate a number of things that should be done to mitigate these. "We call for an adequate understanding of the nature of law. We call on all citizens to take an active concern in the public affairs proper to them. We call on all to examine their conscience and his motives in all his associations with his fellows....."

The whole thing ended with the entreaty. "We ask that each of you shall renew in himself the full meaning of the call which has inspired our people to their highest tasks and in these days of imminent danger: **FEAR GOD, HONOUR THE KING.**"

It was quite a document, and the cast of signatories was very prestigious and most impressive. And it got enormous publicity all over the nation. As you will see below, it brought forth a lot of newspaper correspondence that was fully supportive of it. Indeed, it would have been difficult to argue against any part of it. Having said that, I think it widely missed its mark if it was aimed at changing the behaviour and the way of thinking of loads of Australians.

It was the very fact that there was nothing to argue with that was its weakness. It was full of platitudes, and homilies delivered from thousands of pulpits across the nation Sunday after Sunday, and which themselves were boring the pants off people, and causing church numbers to drop sharply. It had been laboriously constructed by a committee of churchmen, careful not to offend anyone, and who were conscious of the widely divergent audience that they were addressing. It was an extremely difficult document to construct, and the final product showed that.

I add that I admire the people who were behind this. They stuck their necks out and tried to right wrongs that were obvious to them. But from my vantage point over 60 years away, what they were saying was that times were changing, and that they wanted them not to change. The dangers they were talking about were the secularisation of society, and their old bug-bear of modernity, and these were not seen as dangers by the bulk of the community. In any case, here are some typical Letters. You might like to see for yourself the extent to which the authors of the missive on the one hand, and the population who read it on the other, are speaking the same language.

Letters, A Kay. One cannot blame the people for a lack of interest in the Call. They have been experiencing blackouts, shortages of food and other commodities, growing costs of living, and all the restrictions on the existence and enterprise which seven Governments and their attendant departments can impose.

That we have managed to carry on at all is a tribute to the endurance and faith of every Australian. To tell him to wake up to the danger that he is in at home is to warn him of something he is already well aware of, namely, the danger of having the very heart spirit taken out of him by frustration and opposition to all he wants to do and be.

The State is all powerful, and is doing what the individual should be doing, and is doing it badly. The citizen today cannot find an outlet or commensurate reward in enterprise and effort. He sinks back into the organised, massed community, getting food and shelter and limited leisure at the price of his manhood and independence. So he seeks the synthetic emotionalism of Hollywood, and the escape into sport, or any avenue which will aid the forgetting of his frustration.

To make a call to citizens in such circumstances is like a call to prisoners to come out of gaol with the doors locked, the bars up, and the warders alert.

Letters, John Hurley. This great challenge will surely sort out the community. On the one hand the patriots, the down-to-earth thinkers, the genuine Australians, will get in behind it. On the other hand, the real wreckers, who work diabolically against all the principles enunciated, with whom are allied the indifferent and the "smarties," the self-centred minority who see no political gain for themselves, and the starry-eyed impressionables who'd follow a red rat into any trap because some fantastic cause seemed to be at stake, will immediately hurl abuse, and sneer and draw herrings across the track of this move to raise Australia from the doldrums into which it is sliding.

This Call stresses the need to do something we have been failing to do. That is, with honest intent, to pitch in and help. To help one another, the worker, the boss and the firm. It inspires us to take hold on to what we know in our minds to be the better way. That is, to work, plan, and live squarely for the sake of the country.

Letters, J Prendergast. I'm afraid the Call will fail to reach the people. Since the end of the War, there has been prosperity coupled with acute shortages of many essential foods, building materials, etc. Rackets have grown up all over the place. Honest dealing has given way to key-money, black-marketeering, hoarding, and other forms of greed and self-interest. The people have looked to their Governments, and they have looked in vain. Unless something is done soon to clear up the mess, it will be too late.

Letters, CURIOUS. The reasons for their Call exists not so much in their concern for this problem, but in their failure to arrest what they consider the increasing godlessness and lawlessness of the average Australian.

If people are intellectually and morally apathetic, and I suggest that they are not at all, surely there are reasons which catch-cries and cant phrases cannot gloss over. Why are not genuine attempts made to discuss the causes of mental and moral apathy, and genuine solutions put forward?

Letters, John Heffernon. It cannot be generally accepted that the people as a whole are equally responsible for our country's Christian and moral decline, even though, without a doubt, the Call is all-embracing. The responsibility for our decadence rests heavily upon our politicians and businessmen. Many of our laws are totally inadequate and fail to protect the community. Business ethics have declined, and exploitation within and without the law is rampant.

Letters, ANTI-HUMBUG. After two wars and a depression, people can see before them either a third world war or a depression.

What are they to do? Where are they to look? Certainly not the Archbishops. They may be spiritual leaders of those who attend their churches, but nothing more. And the Chief Justices. People look to them to maintain the integrity of our legal system. Are they also good judges of our morals?

Finally, if we respond hysterically to every call made with some air of authority, will we be better off than the Communists or the Fascists?

Letters, A Penfold. The rapid decline in our Christian values and business ethics will not be halted by exhortation, but by example. The yardstick by which success is measured in this country is in terms of money. No matter by what means it has been acquired. Those who have adhered to strict moral principles are now numbered among the new poor.

It is obvious, therefore, that with these facts daily before them, the present generation is hardly likely to follow the road that leads to poverty. They will naturally follow the example that is ever before them, and which leads quickly to success. What incentive is there for them to do otherwise?

There would appear to be something radically wrong with our present system. It is no wonder that many thinkers favour an entirely new social order.

Letters, Marie Irvine. Surely, if there was any further proof needed of the necessity of the Call, it has been supplied by the string of carping Letters which have appeared.

A fundamental fault of Australian people is that they are prepared to find fault with everything. But not one in a hundred has anything constructive to offer. It might be a good starting point if we, as a nation, could correct this weakness.

OVERSEAS NEWS

Negotiators in **Korea** had not improved. They had moved a small distance to a new site, but they haggled and took umbrage and walked out day in and day out. They had, more or less, reached agreement on where a ceasefire line was to be. But that cease-fire was still a long way off. The real problem, one that they had not put fully on the table, was if they called a ceasefire, how could they keep the departing armies from returning any time they liked? Surely, the hawks were arguing in Washington, it would be better to wipe out the Red army completely, and thus remove the problem. On this issue, there was still a lot to be done.

Persia. The Brits had removed everyone from Abadan, and were making pleas to the UN. The UN, completely divided, said it would give a judgement in six weeks time on who should have what out of the carve-up. So Britain was left with the question of what, if anything it could do.

Then, Churchill won the elections, and he said he was prepared to re-open negotiations with Persia. In the meantime, toward the end of November, social unrest in Persia in the form of rioting and looting was increasing daily, and there were growing doubts as to whether Mussadeq could control his more ardent and extreme forces. Things were only middling.

Egypt. Every day, the British or the Egyptians did something to annoy each other, and this mainly resulted in a few lives lost daily. Other nations round the edges of Egypt were getting nervous, and were making military gestures. So, here, things were not quite middling. They were more at the muddling stage. Or perhaps, the meddling stage. But certainly not yet at middling.

SYDNEY VERSUS MELBOURNE

Letters, Densley Waight, Potts Point. As a regular diner-out in both Sydney and Melbourne, may I be permitted to contradict the article of your expert on Melbourne's restaurants.

While some small cafes may have closed during the past year, all of the well-known resorts are continuing with even bigger business than before. Perhaps your expert does not know that within the area of a city block at the top end of Bourke Street are seven first-class Italian restaurants, seating a total of around 1,000, all with male service and menus equalling the world's best. Here it is possible to buy a three-course lunch for five shillings consisting of soup, spaghetti, gnocchi, ravioli or canneloni, and fish or entrée.

As far as this type of menu is concerned, I fail to notice anything but the best cuts of meat in generous quantities exceeding the serves of Sydney. Furthermore, most of them give diners linen serviettes, a Sydney rarity. In the matter of Chinese food, Melbourne also shows prices much below Sydney with appointments of the most modern kind, and music in the largest.

So far as a cheap snack is concerned, most hotels in the city serve lunches in their bars, while one has a lounge where a glass of beer with an ample helping of fresh sandwiches cost two shillings.

It might be pointed out that most of the city's hotels dining-rooms, and every hotel has a good one, supply splendid meals, from a moderate cost to the expensive types in the larger **caravanserais.**

Might I suggest that your expert should pay a visit to modern Sydney, where fifty Shillings is the usual charge for dinner with a bottle of wine. Should he be hungry or thirsty after midnight in Sydney, let me tell him that he will find none of those comfortable and happy all-night cafes that are still part of the night-life of Melbourne and St Kilda.

Comment. In case you missed the point, Densley Waight is extolling the virtues of Melbourne, and contrasting that lucky place with miserable Sydney, which had none of the good things mentioned. But, wait. There is a response, that turns the tables. A Champion has entered the lists.

Letters, E White, Randwick. I do not agree that Melbourne is better to eat in than Sydney.

Recently, in an Italian restaurant in which the elite in Melbourne is supposed to dine, I paid 70 shillings for four people, plus 10 shillings for a bottle of wine . The place was grimy and congested. Our food was mediocre and badly served on small, thick plates.

In Sydney, on the other hand, at some of our night club restaurants, a pleasing four-course dinner, and beautiful surroundings, with sweet music, a lengthy floor-show and dancing, can be had for eight shillings. Five of us dined splendidly from 6 pm till 9.30 pm for a total of sixty shillings, and saw an excellent floor show.

Comment. I go along with Densley Waight. Sydney did have some good nightclubs, and a few good restaurants. Perhaps a dozen, all up. But it had none of the other venues that were described for Melbourne.

NEW AND VIEWS

Letters, L Browne. The traffic authorities altered the central traffic line on Sydney Harbour Bridge by painting it red. Last night was my first experience of this line on a wet night, and I found I could not readily see it. In my opinion, it is dangerous. I suggest that reflectors be placed at intervals along the line. They are most effective.

Letters, R Atkins. I have been very surprised to notice the prevalence of the habit of spitting. I have read in serious literature that if this habit could be stopped, then TB could be wiped out in ten years.

Anyone familiar with the treatment of TB knows that the destruction of sputum from sufferers is of first importance. Could not a publicity campaign against spitting be conducted?

Letters, J Matheson. More British settlers have come to Australia this year than in any previous year. At the same time that permanent departures from the country numbered about 20,000 per year. There can be little doubt that the vast majority of these were caused by the impossibility of securing reasonable accommodation.

I, for one, have had to pay nine Pounds per week for two rooms to house my wife and three children. After nearly two years, their welfare is forcing me to return home. Much as we love Australia and like its people, the adventure, started with so much spirit and hope, has come to nought, and will cost me all my capital.

Do politicians and the people of Australia ever think of the misery and loss involved in these cold figures? Surely British migration is not encouraged, and a cynical calculation is made that at least some migrants will stay?

DECEMBER NEWS ITEMS

A man you have never heard of , **George Henry Powell**, aged 71, died a few days ago. He wrote the WWI song *"Pack up your troubles in your Old Kit Bag"*. The song made him a fortune in royalties.

Princess Elizabeth and Prince Phillip were made members of the highest Court in the land, **the Privy Council.** To show their allegiance to the King, they each kissed his hand. They were, however, excused from taking the oath of allegiance because of their exalted status. **Comment.** All very quaint. Do such practices still prevail?

London. Twenty three cadets, aged about 13, were killed as they marched along a country lane when a double-decker bus ploughed into them. **They were all bandsmen in the Army**, and were marching along to their own music. Eighteen others were injured.

A man before his time. A woolgrower from Victoria, Ted Humphreys, is currently **recruiting top-level tennis players,** mainly recently retired, **to go on tour under** his management. They **will play tennis against each other** in many big cities of the world, and be rewarded by getting prizes for winning.

Comment. At the same time, an American past-champion, Jack Kramer, was forming his own circus, and **this** group **did travel the world for a decade.** Mr. Humphries' tour did not eventuate, **but he wished that one day "open tennis" would become established. His wish did eventually come true.**

Authorities in the **US Army in Tokyo are fed up with fat soldiers**. According to a memorandum from a Brigadier in a high position "I am fed up with excessive overweight and corpulent personnel. That is, those soldiers who are **flabby, soft, seam-busting, bulging-at-the-middle types** who are over-eating and not exercising." His command will not become a haven for gluttons and lounge-addicts.

US news report. In Chicago, a woman was found frozen in the street. **Her body temperature was 64 degrees**, well below the normal human temperature of 98 degrees. She was breathing three times a minute, versus the normal 22. Doctors cut a hole in her throat, gave her cortisone and plasma. **She responded and her temperature is now normal....**

If she recovers, it is likely that she will lose both legs and arms. Footnote: **the lowest body temperature previously recorded was 68 degrees, induced by Nazi doctors in concentration camp experiments.**

The police excelled themselves with an unusual raid. **They arrested a launch** *Lady Brayton* **as it cruised** Sydney Harbour and charged the 60 men on board with playing two-up. **Three police launches** were involved, three **black marias were waiting** at the dock for taking the villains, and **40 police were involved** in the operation. Clearly, this costly raid was not to catch these particular gamblers, but to send a message that no one gambling is safe from the law.

Bakers in Sydney and Melbourne have stated that they will only **deliver bread to the front gate of houses. Also,**

that money for payment must be left at the gate. This was because, in these prosperous times, people cannot be found to cart bread. **Comment.** What a bonanza for the quick-footed petty thief.

Good old Sydney had another cross to bear. Milk was in short supply. **Home delivery was still universal**, and last week, homes got only half their ration. This week, they will get two-thirds.

At Portland, near Lithgow in NSW, **limestone was being mined and crushed into pebbles**, and pushed into a very large tank. It was 40 feet high, with a circular radius of about the same. It had a three feet hole at the bottom to release the pebbles....

A worker, doing maintenance on the wall of the tank, **stood on the pebbles, and started to sink**. He was gradually sucked down as if in quicksand, and **suffocated as he sank**. His dead body was discovered when **his feet appeared though the release hole** at the bottom of the tank.

The world was starting to change. People were throwing off the pre-war acceptance of the status quo, and realising that **great changes were possible**. So, for example, there was a slow-growing idea that **one-brand service stations might work**. And that the tight **dead-hand of the current owners** could be broken if the petrol companies had control of sites.

There was also the growing realisation that the new kid on the block, **automation**, might help workers find a better way of life. So that, demands for a 40-hour week started to go hand in hand with higher productivity considerations. **Maybe it was possible to work only 40 hours and still meet the nation's needs.**

The Letters columns of the newspapers were filling up with protestors who wanted to put **Christ back into Christmas.** "Filling children's heads with Santa, reindeer and holly, and soppy songs will put Christ into the background, and leave us with **a pagan festival.**"

One-man buses are just coming onto the public agenda. In Sydney, on December 12th, three drivers and no conductors were rostered to start a shift on these buses. They will **strike** and other drivers will do the same when told to do so....

The reason is that everyone knows that **reductions in the workforce will happen** when crews are cut from two to one. This is a battle that will rage here, and in the other States, over several years. In the long run of course, **the buses will be accepted.**

In the US, insurance companies are relying on the statement of the President to press their case that the war in **Korea "is a United Nations' police action, and not a war."** If it **is** a war, the insurance companies will be forced to pay compensation for some deaths.

Comment. If it is not a war, I wonder what a war would look like.

Second comment. I was in Melbourne on Christmas Eve of 1951, and thousands of women were doing their last-minute shopping.

That, I suspect, is what real war looked like.

10 MOVIES RELEASED:

Show Boat	Kath Grayson Howard Keel
A Streetcar Named Desire	Vivien Leigh Marlon Brando
Quo Vadis	Robert Taylor Deborah Kerr
African Queen	HumphreyBogart Kath Hepburn
Comin' Round the Mountain	Bud Abbott Lou Costello
Strangers on a Train	Farley Grainger
Lavender Hill Mob	Alec Guinness
An American in Paris	Gene Kelly
Place in the Sun	Elizabeth Taylor
Born Yesterday	Judy Holliday
People will Talk	Cary Grant

ACADEMY AWARDS:

Best Actor   : Humphrey Bogart

Best Actress : Vivien Leigh

Best Movie   : An American in Paris

ENTERTAINMENT

Hit songs from America:

If	**Perry Como**
Be My Love	**Mario Lanza**
Too Young	**Nat King Cole**
Come On-a My House	**RoseM'y Clooney**
Cold, Cold Heart	**Tony Bennett**
Cry	**Johnny Ray**
Gone Fishin'	**Bing Crosby**
Jezabel	**Frankie Laine**
Rose, Rose, I Love You	**Frankie Laine**
My Heart Cries For You	**Dinah Shore**
Hey Good Lookin'	**Hank Williams**
Because of You	**Kelly Clarkson**
I Get Ideas	**Louis Armstrong**
I'm in the Mood	**Johnny Hooker**
Kisses Sweeter than Wine	**The Weavers**
A Kiss to Build a Dream on	**Louis Armstrong**
Taxi Blues	**Little Richard**

TIDYING UP

Korea wrap-up. I always get a bit light-headed as I get close to the end of a book. It seems I am writing these books at more than one a year, and so if I go on for another fifty years doing that, I will get ahead of the years and will be writing about the future. Now that sounds quite interesting, and it seems like I might do just that. I'll wait and see how I feel at the time.

This year, in my light-headed moments, I will indulge myself by talking over some personal thoughts about the Korean War. You will have noticed, as I went through the months, that I got less and less tolerant of what was happening in Korea. So now, I will use up my self-granted indulgence to give you some background to this.

It all started with WWII. I was five years old at the beginning, and only eleven at the end. For me, it was a period that was full of news, and drama, and fear and chaos, and excitement, and everything. As a young boy with a vivid imagination, I was always in the thick of it. I dreamed and day-dreamed of single-handedly wiping out hordes of Krauts and Japs with grenades and machine guns, and with the wonderful Spitfires that I flew so fearlessly. I was certainly the most decorated soldier and airman and seaman in the Aussie Forces, and many times won the adulation of the entire nation for my exploits. Though, as you quite well know, my main aim was to impress June Brown, the primary-school black-headed beauty in the navy sailor-suit. I can remember vividly even now the joy I got from snatching June out from Hiroshima just before that Bomb went off.

When the end of the War came, I was just a little sad in a way, because the need to save the nation had now gone. But, miraculously, there came a need to beat England and India and the West Indies at cricket, and also a whole range on countries at Rugby and tennis and golf. I also had to win several Melbourne Cups, and take much Gold home from the Olympics. So, actually, I was to be kept quite busy doing wonderful things.

In any case, when the Korean War started five years later, I was, not surprisingly, five years older. But I was still just as patriotic as I had ever been. I loved Australia, and I loved the British Empire. Whatever these countries decided to do, I was certain was the right and the sensible thing to do, and I was fully behind them. So I went into this War all gung-ho. I wasn't planning to be **so** active as I had been in the earlier combats, but still I was prepared to serve if called upon in an emergency.

But in that five year period, I had grown in an unusual way. I had progressively developed an interest in politics, and civics, and the world around me. I am happy to say that I was a normal boy, who played footy, and loved cricket, and hated the violin, and broke his arms a few times. There was nothing unusual there. But I was a bit different in one respect. When other boys were reading the *Boys' Champion*, I too was reading the *Boys Champion*. But afterwards I would be reading, analytically and critically, the *Common Cause* or *The Tribune* or the *Bulletin*. There was no sort of reward for this, no one even noticed it. It was just something I did.

So, as I said earlier, when the Korean War came, I, as a serious-minded 16-year-old, thought it was for the benefit of the world, and that it was another example of good about to triumph over evil. I was a little puzzled because I could find no convincing reason for the War starting in the first place, because I could not figure out why the two parts of the one nation would suddenly hate each other so much as to go to war. Still, they were already hard at it, so now all we had to do was win it.

But over the months, as this War developed, so too did my disquiet. I got tired of the military advances and retreats, I was exasperated by MacArthur's cavalier approach, and I was aghast at the farcical negotiations that continued while just a few miles away men were being killed daily by the hundreds. You, the reader, will have seen these attitudes developing month by month as this book progressed, and I think I am accurate in saying that was how these ideas evolved in me at the time.

So by the end of 1951, I was a changed person in my world-wide political thinking. I no longer believed that the West was always right, and the others always wrong. I did not agree that using military force was a good way to solve problems. And I did not trust the men who were leading the nations and the military forces. I grew up quite a lot in that one year.

I was not the only one thus negatively affected by this War. The public in general turned off, and did not want to know about it. From the middle of the year, all the newspapers were calling it the "Forgotten War." Over the final six months of the War, the *Sydney Morning Herald* did not carry a single Letter voicing comments on War policy or events. When the Diggers returned to Australia, and right up until the present day, they and their families complained that they were "Forgotten Soldiers". They rightly objected to the Government's tight-fisted attitude towards them and their war-induced maladies. To the average citizen, there was **no** threat from **overseas** Communism at this stage, and in a time of considerable prosperity, it was a folly to be fighting a far-away "civil" war over some country that they had hardly heard of.

Closing comment. My moments of capriciousness have gone. As usual, at this stage, I will sleep on what I have written, and in the morning, decide whether to actually include it in the book. If I decide against inclusion, you might wonder at the three blank pages that will be there in their stead. If I don't, you might also wonder at the three pages filled with ……. well …. you decide.

CHRISTMAS CHEER

This year the newspapers have had a wonderful time. There has been a welter of serious news, some of it pretendedly frightening, and lots of other news with a high political content. This is all very good for the selling of newspapers.

But now that December has rolled around, the newspapers have moved to a more jovial tone, the impending disasters have suddenly lost their cogency, and instead all eyes are turned towards promoting Christmas.

So, getting into the spirit of things, I will regale you with news of Santa and All Things Christmas.

Letters, Abe Winters. What has happened to Santa Claus? In my childhood, too far away, I remember him as an amiable old gentleman who liked his beard to be tugged at by the poor and those hungry for happiness. He had no part in fifty-guinea dolls, and mechanical toys from ten guineas to the sky.

Where is he now? Has he, at last, been slain by Moloch?

Letters, D Giblin. There can be few thinking people who have not recognised the increasing tendency to push Santa Claus, with his reindeer, snow, holly, and bag of presents, to the fore to such an extent that many, especially small children, cannot see past his beard.

The drama, the excitement, the incredible message of Christmas, is that God, because He loved us, became a man like us and lived with us. The shift of emphasis from this to the traditional accessories, if continued, will rob Christmas of its Christ, and leave us with a pagan festival.

Comment. In case you haven't noticed, **the drive for sales at Christmas** has got a lot worse. But now, to a most serious Santa matter that took up many pages of newspapers in the week before Christmas.

News item, December 18th. The ABC's programme today, Kindergarten of the Air, upset many mothers and children when it broadcast an interpretation of the role of Santa Claus in providing presents for children at Christmas.

In a story prepared by Miss Joan Lennartz, a kindergarten teacher, she told of the activities of young Santa, and how he came to distribute presents to his parents as an adult. This was harmless fanciful kindergarten fare, but then she went on:

Sometimes we **play** that he comes in the night and puts our presents on Christmas trees, so you see mothers and fathers all over the world want to make their children happy and give them things, but they do not always want the children to know who gives the beautiful gifts. They say St. Nicholas, or Santa Claus, must have sent them.

Miss Lennartz professed innocence of any deliberate attempt to undermine the Christmas myth. She pointed out that the story had been prepared in conjunction with the handbook of the Australian Kindergarten College, and she completely denied any connection with terrorist groups. The ABC's General Manager, Charles Moses, described the story as presented as being "quite delightful", and pointed out that his grandchildren would be five years old in a few years, and that he would have no objection to them hearing the story then. He was not at all perturbed by the newspaper photos of women in Melbourne crying bitterly, and in fact he arranged for a re-play of the story to be made in prime time the next evening.

By then, the Letters were pouring in. Here is a sample.

Letters, A Jobson. No one who has seen the faces of small children first thing on Christmas morning will be able to excuse the ABC broadcast, exploding the existence of Father Christmas.

Life is too real and earnest these days for grown-ups, but that is no reason why small children should be made to put aside the fantasies of childhood.

Who among us, remembering his own childhood, cannot recall the joy we found from this grand old man, who exuberates the spirit of Christmas.

Kindergarten teachers do excellent work and no one appreciates more than I do what they have done for my children, but surely they should not try to interfere with home influences.

Whether Father Christmas is to be allowed to exist is surely a matter solely for parents to decide, and not for people who know children only in the classroom. Surely everyone knows that Santa is something that children will grow to realise is a myth. They do not realise it suddenly.

Letters, T McPherson. Congratulations to Miss Lennartz. If we teach a belief in Santa, we are teaching a lie. Does that mean we can teach lies all the time. Can we teach that Hitler was a good man? Can we teach that Communism is beneficial to us? Can we teach that there is no God?

We cannot say it is alright to tell the truth some times, and not at others. Children will not trust their teachers.

Letters, Lorna Wise. When a child definitely asks for the truth about Santa Claus his mind is ready to receive the explanation, which should be given in carefully chosen words.

To suggest that older generations lost faith in adults over this question is pure nonsense, as any who retain the love of fairy tales know.

It is outrageous that such a broadcast should have taken place in a British country.

Letters, L Trevor. It would seem that people today are losing all commonsense about Santa and Christmas.

Child psychologists may be, as Mr Moses says, "experts and know what they are talking about." Well, they may be experts, but they certainly do not know what they are talking about. They do not understand that a fairy tale or a myth is poetry, an effort of the imagination. It gives a feeling that such a story **should** be true in the mind if not in fact.

The fairy godmother **ought** to turn the pumpkin into a coach. Father Christmas **ought** to come down the chimney.

The whole point of the story in my childhood was that he must not be seen or he would go away. Do these people really believe that a child will lose his trust and confidence in beloved parents because in time he will know that Santa Claus is only a beautiful story?

Letters, R Garran. Aren't we taking our aunties too seriously when we suppose that a talk or two can get children to disbelieve what they want to believe. In children's minds there is no clear boundary between imagination and belief.

They are not as easy to hoodwink as might be supposed. Many of them know in their hearts that Daddy is behind Father Christmas's white beard, but they do not want to spoil the fun by telling him so. Play-acting to them is real. How many of us grown-up children know what we believe and what we imagine we believe, or pretend to believe?

How long have wise men and holy men been explaining that leprechauns and the little people are figments of the imagination? Be comforted, parents and professional Father Christmases. There is nothing the radio aunties can do about it.

Letters, Old Clausian. If the "experts" of the Kindergarten of the Air take such a serious view of the perpetuation on the age-old myth of Santa Claus, why do they continue to perpetuate the un-truth, surely of equal iniquity, of stories of talking animals or railway locomotives, and the like, with which children are constantly entertained in the sessions.

Let them be consistent at all costs!

The question of whether or not children should be brought up in the Santa Claus tradition is surely a matter for the parents. If such decisions are to be taken out of their hands, what guarantee have we that some misguided "expert" will not impart un-authorised teaching on religion or sex by medium of the radio?

Letters, REM. It is a nice state of affairs when a secret shared by thousands of parents should be wrested from them by the ABC broadcasting it.

The story was nothing short of impudence. It is not the business of the ABC to take over parents' duties.

Comment. In my own case, I was always frightened that if I admitted I did not believe in Santa, then my parents would stop giving me all those Christmas goodies. Thus, while I am sad that my parents have now departed, I am happy to say they did so in the belief that their very grown-up son still believed in Santa.

NICE THINGS FOR CHRISTMAS

French nylon gloves. The sweetest, most Christmassy gloves anywhere are the genuine French nylon gloves at Lipton's Gift Store. Frilled short ones of fine mesh nylon in white and black are seventeen shillings. In pretty pastel shades, eighteen shillings. Frilled short gloves of plain nylon in white, pastels and black are 23 shillings. Elbow-length gloves of very, very fine mesh, with frilled tops, in white, pastels and black are 32 shillings. There's also a good variety of nylon stockings, imported kid gloves, handbags, elegant long umbrellas and beautiful costume jewellery. Lipton's Gift Store.

Gifts for homemakers. At "Chesterfield Furniture" in George Street you'll notice attractively arranged among the larger pieces of furniture, an extraordinarily interesting collection of small pieces that would make delightful Christmas gifts. Outstanding are these table lamps with Wedgwood figurine bases and silk shades – 15 pounds 10 shillings, and Swiss two-tune musical cigarette boxes with pirouetting ballerina – 10 pounds 5 shillings. Distinctive, too, Swiss chalet musical boxes from three pounds; Wedgwood wall-vases in tulip and mailed-fist designs; Italian hand-painted miniatures and tiny English and Dutch reproductions of antique copper and brass ware. Chesterfield Furniture.

Shantung coat special.   Chatterton's offer of shantung duster coats at the wonderful, little price of five pounds, is beautifully timed for the holidays. We called in to see them the moment the news reached us. They're really most attractive summer coats cut on straight lines with a flare to the back. In the style we favour there's beige and aqua only – but there are oddments also in junior navy and black. Sizes are XSSW to W. If you're unable to call you may send your order by mail to Chatterton's.

A holiday in town. For women who are troubled with facial hairs or moles, a holiday in town provides the opportunity of having these worrisome blemishes removed for all time. At Sister Vimard's Salon, facial hairs and moles are removed in complete privacy under the supervision of a trained nursing sister who has been doing this specialised work for years. Her modern, short-ray method is quick, permanent, ever so gentle and it leaves not the faintest mark or scar. The net result is a younger, fresher look. Sister Vimard.

Last minute gifts can be quickly chosen from the wonderful variety of hand-worked linens and laces at Aginian's – doyleys, guest towels, tray cloths, supper cloths, table mats, serviettes….from the Chinese novelties – slippers, fans, gloves and dolls. Then, often, just before Christmas you'll suddenly remember half a dozen people you should have bought gifts for. You'll find that having a small stock of handkerchiefs is a great help. Aginian's have very lovely handkerchiefs this year, boxed or loose, of handworked Irish linen, at a wide range of prices from three shillings.

There's a prettier way to wear your hair – and that's the way you'll want it for your Christmas parties. All this season's hair styles are very soft and pretty; but there's one version that will flatter your looks particularly. Mr Borrowman and his staff of Continental experts are quick to see what style will be exactly right for you. For a summer permanent they recommend the Ondulux Machineless or the Zero Cool Wave – and there's still time to have it before Christmas. J D Borrowman, MIT (London).

SUMMING UP 1951

The year that was. At the end of the year, economic conditions were not quite as buoyant as they were at the start. The price of wool and agricultural commodities was down a bit, and the Government had introduced a credit squeeze which upset anyone wanting to borrow money. This hurt people who wanted a loan for a home or a car, and anything on hire purchase. So the nation was not as prosperous as before, but still things were not at all bad, and it could reasonably be hoped that things would improve with a little sweating.

The Government was settling down a bit. When the Government changes hands, in this case from Labor to Liberal, it always comes in with a rash of new initiatives. Then after a while, it has to deal with the consequences of these new measures, and begins to spend increasing time on handling the problems that were thus created. This was what was happening at the end of 1951, and most people were happy that it was. No one wants to be on edge all the time, worried that government might change the status quo. So a period of quiescence in Canberra was welcome.

Internationally, the Korean war was still around, but this seemed not to be a real war. The next major event on the war calendar was the minor Egyptian war of 1956, and then the Vietnam war of the sixties. But these were a long way off, and people were getting less paranoid about overseas conflicts, and were more intent on enjoying the world of the Baby Boom.

So, at the end of 1951, this nation was happily prosperous. No one could say he didn't have a worry in the world, because everyone always enjoys some worries. But if you go back ten years to 1941, this nation, already at war in Europe, had just been forced into the war with Japan. That fact makes the worries of 1951 seem trivial by comparison. So, if you were lucky enough to be born in 1951, I expect that got you off to a good start, and I hope that continued throughout your entire life.

Born in 1943?
What else happened?
Australian Social History
Ron Williams

In 1943, Prime Minister Chifley went on to introduce butter, clothing, and meat rationing. But he allowed most workers a week's holiday at Christmas. And the blackout covers on all windows could be removed. Though they had to go up again. Zoot suits and fights in city pubs were very popular especially if they involved USA servicemen. But fears of Japanese invasion had gone by year's end.

Born in 1944?
What else happened?
Australian Social History
Ron Williams

In 1944, the Japs in the Pacific and the Nazis in Europe were just about beaten. Sydney was invaded by rats and Yankee soldiers were in all our cities. Young girls were being corrupted by the Yanks and by war-time freedom, and clergy were generous with their advice to them.

****

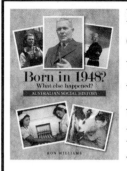

In 1948, there was no shortage of rationing and regulation, as the Labor government tried to convince voters that war-time restrictions should stay. Immigration Minister Calwell was staunchly supporting our White Australia Policy, though he would generously allow five coloured immigrants from each Asian nation to settle here every year. Burials on Saturday were banned. Rowers in Oxford were given whale steak to beat meat rationing.

****

AVAILABLE FROM ALL GOOD BOOK STORES AND NESWAGENTS